BUSINESS

COMMUNICATION

Topics & Activities

Second Edition

Richard D. Featheringham
Nancy Csapo

KENDALL/HUNT PUBLISHING COMPANY
4050 Westmark Drive   Dubuque, Iowa 52002

ABOUT THE AUTHORS

Dr. Richard D. Featheringham is a professor in the Business Information Systems Department at Central Michigan University, Mount Pleasant, Michigan, teaching courses in business communication, business report writing, and business ethics.

Dr. Featheringham has given presentations on the national and international level and has researched, written, and consulted extensively in the areas of national and international business communication, business ethics, business information systems, and methodology for teaching.

Dr. Featheringham received the Excellence in Teaching Award from Central Michigan University, the College of Business Administration (CMU) Dean's Teaching Award, the College of Business (CMU) Ameritech Excellence in Teaching Award, the Outstanding Educator of the Year Award from the National Court Reporters Association, the Outstanding Teaching Excellence Award from the Academy of Business Administration, the Mortar Board Outstanding Faculty of the Year, and selected several times for the Who's Who Among America's Teachers award.

Dr. Nancy Csapo is an associate professor in the Business Information Systems Department at Central Michigan University, Mount Pleasant, Michigan. Dr. Csapo is in charge of the undergraduate Business Teacher Education Program at CMU and teaches courses in business communication, business teacher education methods, and computers.

Dr. Csapo enjoys the planning, development, and implementation of creative teaching techniques for both traditional and non-traditional students; the utilization of active learning strategies in the classroom; and the motivation of students to positively impact the quality and delivery of education. She enjoys an active research agenda, including giving presentations at state, national, and international conferences with a primary focus on effective teaching and learning.

Dr. Csapo has received numerous teaching awards, including the Excellence in Teaching Award from CMU, the College of Business Administration (CMU) Dean's Teaching Award, the College of Business (CMU) Ameritech Excellence in Teaching Award, the Outstanding Post-secondary Teacher of the Year Award from the Michigan Business Education Association, and has been selected several times for Who's Who Among America's Teachers.

CONTENTS

UNIT I—EMPLOYMENT COMMUNICATION Page

UNIT II—ORAL COMMUNICATION

UNIT III—WRITTEN COMMUNICATION

APPPENDIX—TEACHING TOOLS AND FORMS Page

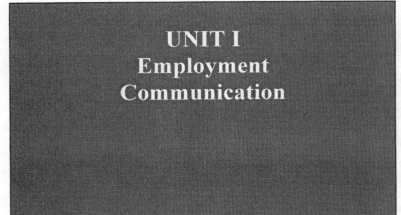 

UNIT I
Employment
Communication

CAPSTONE PROJECT FOR EMPLOYMENT COMMUNICATION UNIT I

The Capstone Project for Unit I is designed to apply the main topics in this unit into one integrated assignment. The integration of the unit topics via the completed assignments will result in an employment resource portfolio that, when completed, will consist of the following:

1. Two versions of your current resume (in chronological and scannable formats).

2. Solicited cover letter for an internship or a job.

3. Unsolicited cover letter for an internship or a job.

4. Thank-you letter for an interview.

5. A letter of recommendation.

6. Letter accepting a position.

7. Letter rejecting a position.

8. A follow-up letter for an application.

9. A two-sided business card.

10. Common interview questions with answers. Prepare your answers for some of the most common interview questions. Refer to the lists at the end of this unit and outline your answers to the questions..

11. Printouts of Internet resources related to employment communication.

Note: An evaluation form is included in the *Appendix,* pages 197-198.

| **TOPIC** | **Chronological resume** (examples pages 8-10) |

| **DEFINITION** | A chronological resume is a document summarizing qualifications and experience for education, employment, and other skills. |

Two common types of resumes:
1. *Chronological resumes* are a common format for resumes emphasizing work experience.
    a. Employment history (and education) is included with the most recent listed <u>first</u>.

2. *Functional resumes* are "achievement oriented" and list qualifications by emphasizing skills and abilities.

| **KEY POINTS** | **(*refer to "Top Ten Resume Mistakes" page 7)** |

1. Resumes must be <u>error free</u> and well organized so that employers can easily spot what they are looking for as they scan your resume.
    a. Approximately 75 percent of employers will remove an applicant for a typo and/or a grammatical error on a resume.

2. Average time an employer spends reviewing your resume is less than two minutes; some estimates are less than one minute.

3. The most readable font size is a 12-point font for the body of your resume; never use smaller than a 10-point font and use a larger font size for your name.

4. Do use a variety of effects (*e.g.,* bold, underline, italics, bullets for lists), but be consistent.

5. Do use an objective <u>if</u> that objective strengthens your resume, if 60 percent of your resume supports it, and if it doesn't limit your opportunities
    a. If you do use an objective, you will probably need to change it for every position for which you apply.

6. Do list education and work experience in reverse chronological order (most recent first).

7. Do use a consistent format for dates when listing work experiences that include <u>month and year</u>.

8. Do not use complete sentences; your resume should be an

2

"outline" of your qualifications and experiences, not a narrative.

9. Do not use personal pronouns such as "I" or "me" in your resume.

10. Do be specific in describing past employment; use parallel phrasing – include the month/year of employment dates, be concise; use past tense for all job duties, *e.g.,* "supervised staff members."

11. Do not list hobbies and/or personal information.

12. Do not include your photo on your resume.

13. Do keep your resume to 1-2 pages in length.
    a. If your resume is two pages, include a header with your name at the top of the second page and the page number (see example two-page resume, pages 9-10).

14. For distributing the resume, use high-quality bond or parchment paper in neutral colors with black ink.

15. For electronic resumes, see scannable resumes, page 12.

FORMAT

Recommended sections and sequence of a chronological resume:
1. Heading (name, address, contact information, including email).

2. Educational background (school name, city/state, degree, major/minor, date completed or *expected* date of completion).
    a. Rule for including GPA or not – if 3.0 or higher (on 4.0 scale) then list it; or only put GPA in your major if above 3.0.

3. Special skills, certifications, or qualifications (*e.g.,* list of computer skills, software applications, related courses or training, areas of expertise, etc.)

4. Employment history, including dates (month/year), job title and duties.

5. Activities, honors/awards, or professional memberships.

6. Use a separate reference page to list your references to give to the interviewer during an interview.

      a. Include "references available upon request" on your resume when mailing.

      b. Recommended number of references to list on your reference page is 3-5 (see example reference page on page 11).

      c. List references in alphabetical order.

STEPS

1. Gather all necessary information-- dates, names, etc.

2. Choose the resume format most appropriate for your situation (chronological or functional) – chronological with education listed first is most common.

3. Find a resume design you like to use in creating your own resume (see examples provided; see "activities" below also).

4. Prepare your resume; proofread the resume many times and always have at least one other person proofread it as well.

ACTIVITIES

1. Finding resume resources:

      a. Visit your university's career services office to find information on designing effective resumes.

      b. Checkout an on-line employment web site to get ideas for resume styles and format ideas for your own resume and to find a posting for a job you feel you would be qualified for when you graduate to make your employment unit capstone project more realistic.

2. Create your chronological resume to include in your employment resource portfolio (part of the Capstone Project for this unit). Proofread your resume several times and have at least one other person proofread it. Remember, your resume must be *perfect!*

3. Create a two-sided business card that you can use for networking at professional and social functions. Print your name, address, and vital statistics on the front of the card. Print a mini resume on the reverse side of the card. Check with your instructor or one of the technicians in the computer lab to see how best to create the business card.

4. Get a consensus in your class as to whether your education or your experience is more likely to impress the recruiter or interviewer. Discuss.

RESOURCES

1. www.jobhuntersbible.com – a supplement to the best selling book *What Color is Your Parachute*; provides access to their extensive library of resources including tests, job-hunting articles and advice, a guide to using the Internet for job searches, and links to employment information.

2. http://campus.monster.com - free service where you can post your resume and search over 1,000,000 job postings; provides 3,000 pages of resume help, salary data, and industry information.

3. www.adguide.com - free service specifically for students and recent graduates where you can post your resume and search thousands of job postings; used to find entry-level jobs, career opportunities and job-seeking help.

4. www.provenresumes.com - resume and job search tips; resume strategies and "rate your resume" quiz.

7. www.collegegrad.com/resumes - a web site devoted to new college grads with sample entry level resumes, cover letters and more.

8. www.careerlab.com/letters/default.htm - provides access to CareerLab's cover letter library.

9. www.headhunter.net/JobSeeker/CRC/Index.htm - Career builder's comprehensive resource center for all areas of the job hunt, preparation, and career assessment.

10. http://www.jobweb.com/Resumes_Interviews/resume_guide/restips.html - guide to resume writing, creating an effective resume, and access to sample resumes.

11. www.Jobsmart.org/tools/resume/index.htm - guide to writing resumes; includes sample resumes and links to resume resources.

12. www.quintcareers.com/cover_letter_samples.html - Quintessential Careers sample dynamic cover letters.

13. www.hotjobs.com – Yahoo's HotJobs web site provides career tools and allows you to search jobs and post resumes.

14. www.thejobresource.com – a service for college students and recent graduates looking for entry level jobs, internships, and other opportunities.

15. www.ajb.dni.us - America's job bank provides career information and career tools, job searches, and much more.

16. www.bestjobsusa.com – find a job, post a resume, employment tips, and career resources.

17. http://content.monster.com/tools - "tools center" for Monster.com web site - determine your workplace competencies and marketable skills by completing numerous career **self-assessment tests** (virtual interviews, career interest inventory, cultural sensitivity, job fit, and more).

18. www.hoovers.com/free/ and www.virtualchase.com/coinfo/ - **Research companies** online before your interview; provides instructions to help you find free company and industry information on the Web including financial data, recent news events, and contact information.

19. www.salary.com – provides **salary** and benefits facts and information; self-tests; links to resume posting sites; computes and compares salaries geographically; and provides access to a wide variety of employment-related articles and resources.

Relocation web sites:

www.homefair.com

www.virtualrelocation.com

www.movingsoon.net

http://relocationcentral.com

The Top Ten Resume Mistakes

A list of the top ten most frequently made mistakes in resume writing:

1. Too long (preferred length is 1-2 pages for recent college graduates).

2. Disorganized information scattered around the page, making it hard to follow.

3. Poorly typed and printed, making it hard to read and looking unprofessional.

4. Overwritten, long paragraphs and sentences, taking too long to say too little.

5. Too sparse, giving only bare essentials of dates and job titles.

6. Not showing enough of what the candidate accomplished on the job.

7. Too many irrelevancies: height, weight, sex, health, marital status is not needed.

8. Misspellings , typographical errors, poor grammar; resumes should be carefully proofread before being printed and mailed).

9. Tries too hard—fancy typesetting and binders, photographs and exotic paper stocks distract from the clarity of the presentation.

10. Misdirected—too many resumes arrive on employers' desks unanswered and with little or no apparent connection to the organization. Cover letters would help avoid this situation.

Taken from *Career Advisor* **at** www.talentfreeway.com/
Adapted from Tom Jackson and Ellen Jackson, *The New Perfect Resume,* **Doubleday Publishing Group, 1996.**

KEVIN MATTHEWS

Current Address:
1820 S. Crawford, Apt. M-320
Mount Pleasant, MI 48858
(989) 555-3000 [until Dec. 18, 2004]

Permanent Address:
12225 Ashley
Clinton Township, MI 48038
(810) 555-1212

EDUCATION	**CENTRAL MICHIGAN UNIVERSITY,** Mount Pleasant, Michigan Bachelor of Science in Business Administration, December 2004 Major: *Marketing* Minor: *Spanish* GPA: 3.1(4.0) overall
COMPUTER SKILLS	Word Perfect Excel Word Access
INTERNSHIP 5/2003 – 8/2003	**THYSSEN STEEL GROUP,** Detroit, Michigan **Intern,** *Customer Service Department* • Placed international calls, translated faxes and correspondence • Provided product information to customers • Gained experience in import – export operations • Worked with distribution department to expedite orders
WORK EXPERIENCE 9/2004 - present	**CENTRAL MICHIGAN UNIVERSITY,** Mount Pleasant, Michigan **Office Assistant,** *Alumni & Development Office* • Provide clerical assistance throughout academic year • Prepare mailings for university activities • Participate in annual phone-a-thon fundraisers • Assist in training new student workers
5/2001 – 4/2003	**J. C. PENNEY,** Mount Clemens, Michigan **Sales Associate** • Developed thorough product knowledge base • Handled money and operated computerized cash register • Honored as "Associate of the Month" for July 2002
5/1999 – 8/2000	**ELIAS BROTHERS' BIG BOY,** Mount Clemens, Michigan **Wait Staff** • Operated cash register and resolved customer complaints • Assisted with new staff orientation • Established excellent rapport with customers, co-workers and management
ACTIVITIES	• American Marketing Association • Sweeney Residence Hall Council Member • Students Against Drunk Driving – President • Campus Ambassador – CMU Admissions Office • Michigan Competitive Scholarship Recipient

Kellie Seritt

1950 North Shore Drive • Port Hope, MI 48468 • (517) 555-5252 • kellieseritt@hotmail.com

Education
Central Michigan University, Mount Pleasant, Michigan
Bachelor of Science in Education – August 2004
Majors: Mathematics (EX)
        Business Education (GX) - Office Concentration (VB)
        Michigan Secondary Provisional Certificate 7-12
GPA: 3.93/4.00 (overall)

Delta College, University Center, Michigan
Associate of Arts – April 2000
GPA: 3.9/4.00 (overall)

- Self-financed 100% of education through scholarships and work

Teaching Experience
Full-time Substitute Teacher - Merrill Community School; Merrill, Michigan
(March – April 2004)
- Taught advanced algebra and Computers 6, 7, and 8
- Created daily lesson plans, individual and group activities, and quizzes
- Incorporated Internet projects and other keyboarding activities
- Graded various work, completed report cards, and held parent/teacher conferences
- Attended Inspiration Software Training and Brain Research Session

Student Teacher - Hemlock High School; Hemlock, Michigan
(January – March 2004)
Supervising Teachers: Mrs. Sheila Hinds, Mr. Robert Jones
- Taught business education service and technology, accounting, and management support
- Incorporated various projects using the Internet into daily lessons
- Created week-long unit teaching Boolean Internet searches
- Ordered examination books for management support and designed two additional projects
- Graded various work and completed report cards
- Attended extra-curricular activities

Substitute Teacher - Huron Intermediate School District; Bad Axe, Michigan
(May – December 2003)
- Taught at various schools in numerous subjects, grades K-12
- Planned and worked with staff to provide daily lessons and activities

9

Related Work Experience

Receptionist - Harbor Beach Resort Association; Harbor Beach, Michigan
(June – August 2002)
- Answered telephone and scheduled reservations
- Calculated daily meal billings and organized meal sheets for wait staff
- Sent out weekly billings and prepared weekly reports
- Monitored various activities including bike rentals, ordering of newspapers, and prioritizing resort requests

Supervisor - The Copy Center; Mount Pleasant, Michigan
(August 2000 – June 2001)
- Supervised 12 customer service representatives in team setting
- Monitored inventory and ordered supplies
- Prepared in-store forms, brochures, and advertising displays

Secretary - Delta College, General Services; University Center, Michigan
(August 1998 – August 2000)
- Prepared numerous office documents including forms, letters, memos, and reports
- Answered telephones, prioritized work orders, and organized documents and files
- Supervised general store, monitored inventory, ordered supplies, calculated daily billings and prepared monthly reports

Scholarships and Awards
- Michigan Competitive Scholarship
- Central Michigan University's Academic Honors Scholarship
- Central Michigan University's Richtmeyer Mathematics Scholarship
- Central Michigan University's Drayton and Minnie Miley Teacher Education Scholarship
- 2-year Basketball Scholarship from Delta College Women's Basketball Program
- Delta College Board of Trustees' Outstanding Graduate Award for obtaining a GPA of 4.00 upon graduation
- Dr. Daniel Kinsey Memorial Award (Delta College) for athletic, scholastic and community achievement

Activities
- Kappa Mu Epsilon Honor Society Member
- Golden Key National Honor Society Member

♦ **References available upon request**

References for
Kellie Seritt

1950 North Shore Drive • Port Hope, MI 48468 • (517) 555-5252 • kellieseritt@hotmail.com

Mrs. Janice Bannister
Sales Manager
Harbor Beach Resort Association
3901 N. Bay Road
Harbor Beach, MI 48468
(517) 555-3131
Email: bann@cmich.edu

Mrs. Sheila Hinds
Supervising Teacher
Hemlock High School
7808 School Drive
Hemlock, MI 48488
(989) 555-2121
Email: shinds45@ cmail.edu

Mr. Robert Jones
Supervising Teacher
Hemlock High School
7808 School Drive
Hemlock, MI 48488
(989) 555-1222
Email: jonesy@cmich.edu

Dr. Ellen Richards
Associate Professor
Mathematics Department
Central Michigan University
Mount Pleasant, MI 48859
(989) 774-4000
Email: erich@yahoo.com

Key Points:
- Use of separate reference page (typically provided at interview)
- 3-5 references listed in alphabetical order
- Complete contact information for each reference provided; including professional title, email address, and phone number

11

| **TOPIC** | Electronic (scannable) resume (example page 14) |

DEFINITION

An electronic or scannable resume uses the basic form of a resume without the formatting elements that are misread by scanners. When a job posting requests your resume be submitted electronically, be sure to send your resume in the proper format (e.g. text or ASCII).

RATIONALE

More and more companies are scanning resumes into their human resource databanks for quick, easy retrieval later and to eliminate the need to store paper copies.

Scanning technology enables employers to retrieve resumes based on **key word searches** for skills and qualifications to help locate qualified candidates. Most common key words for entry level, non-technical jobs are *teamwork* and *customer service*.

How do employers prefer to receive resumes?
- a. 31 percent prefer mail
- b. 34 percent prefer email
- c. 7 percent don't accept email resumes
- d. 7 percent prefer web-based resumes

KEY POINTS

1. Remember - electronic resumes are a "no-frills" version of your resume. Key to scannable resumes is that letters and/or characters do NOT touch. Refer to Monster's tips on scannable resumes at their web site: http://content.monster.com/resume/resources/scannableresume/

2. Use a sans serif font like Arial or Optima (not Times New Roman).

3. Use the same font and font size on the entire document (12-point font recommended, but all fonts are not the same).

4. Use the normal arrangement of upper- and lower-case letters, but never all caps.

5. Be careful when using special formatting such as underlines, vertical or horizontal lines. These formatting options are okay to use as long as the letters and/or do NOT touch each other.

6. Do NOT use ampersands (&) or percent signs.

7. Do NOT use two-column formats or lists in columnar format.

8. Use hyphens in place of bullets, some bullets do not translate correctly and can be misread as characters).

9. Left-justify every line.

10. Space before and after slashes, e.g., PC / Apple

11. Use specific **key words** throughout your resume that will correspond to what employers will search for and that reflect key skills and qualifications.

12. Sending an updated resume is acceptable, but only one time. Include a note stating that the resume has been updated.

13. Use plain white paper <u>only</u> when sending out resumes that will be scanned and <u>do not</u> fold or staple (use 9 x 12 envelopes when mailing; use paper clips).

14. For online resumes, you should include an objective and identify the desired position.

ACTIVITIES

1. Using your chronological resume created in the previous section, convert your chronological resume to an electronic (scannable) resume format to include in your employment resource portfolio (part of the Capstone Project for this unit).

2. Design and print a two-sided business card that you can use for networking at professional and social events. On one side of the card should be your contact information, including: name, address, phone, email, etc. On the other side of the card should be a summarized version of your resume. Refer to page 219 in the *Appendix* for additional information.

RESOURCES

Check out the following web site that provides information about creating scannable resumes:

http://provenresumes.com/reswkshps/electronic/scnres.html

http://www.quintcareers.com/scannable_resumes.html

http://www2.jobtrak.com/help_manuals/jobmanual/scan.html

http://www2.jobtrak.com/help_manuals/jobmanual/scan.html

Samuel Smith

Current address:
2312 My Street
Mount Pleasant, MI 48858
(555) 555-5555

Permanent address:
340 My Drive
Lansing, MI 48909
(555) 555-5555
ssmith@cmich.edu

Objective
Sales or marketing representative; interests in marketing analysis and research.

Education
Central Michigan University, Mount Pleasant, Michigan
B.S., Marketing, May 2004
Overall GPA 3.52/4.0

Relevant skills
Teamwork
Customer service
Interpersonal communications

Employment
Marketing internship, ABC Systems, Inc.
Midland, MI Summer 2003
Provided customer service with direct sales marketing
Established new sales territory

Sales Associate, Mistle's Department Store
Mount Pleasant, MI May 2000 – July 2002
Maintained sales records for reporting purposes
Provided sales training to new associates
Recorded inventory information using in-story computer system

Awards and activities
Dean's List, 5 semesters
Kiwanis Club National Scholarship Recipient, 2000
Students Against Drunk Drivers, 2000 – present

Professional affiliations
American Marketing Association, 2002 – present

| **TOPIC** | **Cover letters (solicited and unsolicited)** |

| **DEFINITION** | A cover letter (sometimes called a letter of application) accompanies a resume when seeking a job interview. A *solicited* cover letter is written when the job is advertised or the applicant *knows* of the job. An *unsolicited* cover letter is written when the applicant *does not know* that a job opening exists. |

KEY POINTS

1. Cover letters are printed on the same quality of paper as the paper used to prepare the resume.

2. Cover letters must be proofread carefully to be 100 percent error free. Have a friend read your cover letter and make suggestions for improvement.

3. Include your return address and email address in your personal letterhead as shown on page 18.

5. Keep your cover letter brief; target the job duties, skills, and requirements listed in the job posting whenever possible.
   a. Follow the cover letter template on page 16 for paragraph content guidelines.

STEPS

1. Refer to the cover letter template on page 17.
   a. Use block format, direct pattern.

2. In the first paragraph of a *solicited* cover letter, tell why you are writing; refer to the specific position, and tell how you heard of the opening. If you are writing an *unsolicited* cover letter, ask a question that will get the reader's attention: "How would you like to hire an employee whose knowledge, interest, and experience in sales are top-notch? Well, I may be the one you're looking for, Ms. Lopez."

3. In the next one or two paragraphs of both a solicited and unsolicited cover letter, discuss one or two of your qualifications as they relate to the qualifications required for this position.
   a. Tell why you are particularly interested in the company, location, and/or type of work.
   b. Point out any related experience, specialized training, or related courses.
   c. Offer any evidence of past employment; mention anything that will give additional information concerning background and interests.

4. In the last paragraph of both a solicited and an unsolicited cover letter, refer the reader to the enclosed resume.
   a. Close by making a specific request for an interview.
   b. Make sure your closing is a call to action.
   c. Show appreciation.

5. Be sure to include the "enclosure" notation to indicate your resume is included.

6. Proofread your finished letter *carefully*.
   a. Proofreading technique—read the letter aloud-- or better yet, find someone else to read the letter aloud to you.

ACTIVITIES

1. Find a specific job posting on the Internet or newspaper to use in preparing your cover letter (part of the Capstone Project for this unit).

   a. Prepare a *solicited* cover letter that addresses the qualifications of the job posting and follows the guidelines outlined in this section.

   b. Be sure to have at least one person proofread your cover letter.

2. Use the Internet or other resource to find samples of cover letters. Discuss your findings with other class members.

3. Write a *solicited* cover letter for an internship position in your major area of study. You will be available to intern any of the next two semesters. Attach a copy of your resume.

4. Re-write the letter in #3 (above) as an *unsolicited* cover letter for an internship position in your major area of study.

Cover Letter Template

Personal Letterhead (your name, address, phone and email)

Date

Key Point:
- Use personal letterhead (see example cover letter p. 18); followed by date

Contact person (use proper name)
Title
Company/address

4 spaces after date line
----
double before and after salutation

Dear _____:

1st paragraph
- *Refer to specific ad (name of paper, date, etc.) by job title*
- *Show knowledge of company/reputation/your desire to work there, etc.*

2nd-3rd paragraph(s)
- *Relate your experiences and focus on your most significant qualifications as they relate to job requirements*
- *Discuss your educational qualifications, computer skills, etc. as relevant*

last paragraph
- *Refer to your enclosed resume; show appreciation*
- *Ask for an interview, refer to main qualifications again (briefly)*

Sincerely,

Your Signature

Your typed name

Enclosure

Key Points:
- Be sure to sign your letter and include the "Enclosure" notation

4 spaces; sign your name in this space
----
double space

17

Roger C. Paulson

2195 Melody Drive • *Mount Pleasant, MI 48858* • *(989) 555-5252* • *paul1rc@cmich.edu*

September 1, 200x

Ms. Amy Doe, CPA
Doe, Hartman, Burgess CPA Firm
834 Exchange Building
Lansing, MI 49873

Dear Ms. Doe:

Professor Maria Gonzales has told me that your firm is looking for a competent staff accountant. With thorough college training in accounting and related studies, varied accounting experience, and proven ability to work efficiently, I feel I can be an asset to your staff.

To prepare adequately for a public accounting career, I have completed 40 hours of accounting coursework at Central Michigan University, with an overall grade-point average of 3.8 (on a 4-point scale). Several management information courses I have completed also have provided me with the knowledge and skills that would be useful in working with your clients who use computers. My studies in speech and business communication enable me to present clearly the financial data and reports for clients.

Since your firm specializes in medical accounts, I believe I can be of special benefit to you because of my interest and work in this area. At my previous position I was preparing weekly payrolls for 60 hospital maintenance employees. The position included keeping time and labor union benefit reports and handling accounts payable.

Please call me at (989) 555-5252 after you have reviewed the enclosed resume. I will be happy to talk with you about being your staff accountant. I am home after 3:30 p.m. each weekday.

Sincerely,

Roger C. Paulson

Roger C. Paulson

Enclosure

Roger C. Paulson

2195 Melody Drive • Mount Pleasant, MI 48858 • (989) 555-5252 • paul1rc@cmich.edu

October 1, 200x

Ms. Constance Wayland
Human Resources Director
Soft Drink Bottling Company, Inc.
9874 West Patriot Street
Punxsutawney, PA 39874

Dear Ms. Wayland:

If you need a person who can make effective sales calls and who can provide imaginative merchandising help, then I am your new employee, Ms. Wayland.

Practical work as a Field Representative for the Sweetwater Cola Company gave me an opportunity to plan and execute sales promotions that sold soft drinks. I have proven ability to open new accounts and secure the best floor displays. I have also conducted route analyses and set up key account systems.

Frequent contact with retailers has been part of my duties since I began selling. I have an excellent working knowledge of trade jargon.

After you have had the opportunity to review my attached resume, please write me frankly whether I should anticipate a career with your company. I will appreciate an opportunity to discuss my qualifications with you any day of the week. Please call me at (989) 555-5555 to schedule an appointment. Please keep my resume on file for future reference.

Sincerely yours,

Susanna M. Hunter

Susanna Macon Hunter

Enclosure

TOPIC   **Thank-you letter**

EXPLANATION   A brief thank-you letter should always be sent after an interview to show appreciation, good manners, and perseverance.

a. Most importantly, a thank-you letter will help you to stand out from other candidates.

b. A traditional letter is still the most common form of a thank-you letter, but email is considered acceptable.

c. Be sure you ask the interviewer for her or his business card to be certain you have the necessary information.

KEY POINTS

1. Send a thank-you letter promptly after an interview (within 24 hours ideally).

2. Refer to the interviewer's business card for correct title, address, and proper spelling of name.

3. If interviewed by more than one person, send a letter to each interviewer.

4. Use the direct pattern-- the first sentence should thank the interviewer for his or her time; refer to the interview date and the specific position for which you interviewed.

5. Mention a topic discussed during the interview, or refer to the positive impression made by some aspect of the interview.

6. Mention a skill or strength you have for the position that you did not have the chance to discuss during the interview.

7. Refer to any recent award or accomplishment that relates to the job requirements that you may have forgotten to mention during the interview.

8. Conclude the letter by restating your interest in the job; if you are no longer interested in the job, now is the time to share this information as well.

STEPS

1. Use proper format outlined on page 22.

2. Use direct pattern and be brief!

ACTIVITIES

1. Interview an employer or human resource professional and ask her or him the following questions:

   a. Do you think it's important that interviewees send thank-you letters? Why? Discuss with other class members.

   b. What percentage of applicants interviewed by you or your company would you estimate sends thank-you letters? Discuss.

2. Create a thank-you letter for an interview based on the job posting you used for your cover letter to include in your employment resource portfolio (part of the Capstone Project for this unit).

   a. Proofread your letter carefully; ask a classmate to proof the letter also.

Patrick Jones
Jonesp07@hotmail.com

1280 Maple Street
Mount Pleasant, MI 48858

April 30, 200x

> Date line is first typed line after letterhead; then 4 returns to name and address of recipient

Ms. Patricia Stevens
Simkins Financial Group
800 Glenview Parkway
Clare, MI 48617

Dear Ms. Stevens:

Thank you for the opportunity to interview with you for the accounting position on Monday, April 29.

I enjoyed learning more about Simkins Financial Group and the accounting department. I was impressed by the friendly atmosphere and enjoyed meeting the accounting staff. The accounting courses I have recently completed were especially relevant to the challenges of a financial services organization.

Now that I have a better understanding of the responsibilities of your accounting department, I am confident that my qualifications and skills would be a real contribution to the team at Simkins Financial Group. My education and work experience in the accounting field have given me the real world experience you seek. I look forward to hearing from you soon.

Sincerely,

Patrick Jones

Patrick Jones

| **TOPIC** | **Letter accepting a position** |

DEFINITION A letter accepting a position with a company should be written when you accept the job.

EXPLANATION A letter accepting a position is considered a "good news" letter.
      a. Use the *direct* style of writing.
      b. Be brief.

STEPS

1. Use personal letterhead with the proper date line, address of the recipient, and salutation.

2. Place the acceptance in the first sentence.

3. Keep the letter short and simple.

4. Close with a positive, forward-looking statement.

5. Be sure to include the "enclosures" notation if including other documents with your letter.

6. Proofread very carefully.
      a. Read the letter aloud; then read the letter to another person.

ACTIVITIES

1. Look at the jobs available advertisements in the recent edition of a local newspaper. Find a job that you think you would like. Assume that you have been offered the job by the company. Write the job acceptance letter.

2. Search the Internet to find a sample of a job acceptance letter. How is the letter the same or different from the one you wrote? Write a memo to your instructor telling he or she what you have found (refer to memo format guidelines in Unit III, pages 93-94).

3. Assume that you have been successful in getting an internship for the next semester. Write a letter accepting the internship to the company who offered that internship to you.

Sarah Moore
moore1sr@cmich.edu

ℳ

2850 Knoll Drive
Lansing, MI 48909

June 1, 200x

Mr. Juan A. Jobb, Manager
Human Resources Division
Jobb Products, Inc.
76 North Bailey Road
Tyler, TX 78900

Dear Mr. Jobb:

I accept, with pleasure, your offer of a job in the Information Systems Division of Jobb Products.

Enclosed is the information you requested from me along with the reference letters from three former employers.

Working for your company has always been a goal of mine; thank you so much for the offer. I look forward to many long years of employment with Jobb Products.

Sincerely,

Sarah Moore

Sarah Moore

Enclosures

TOPIC   **Letter rejecting a position**

DEFINITION

When you receive a job offer that you cannot accept, you should write an indirect (inductive) style letter turning down the job. Be as pleasant as you can because you may one day be looking for another job, and you may want to consider another offer—perhaps one you rejected in the past.

EXPLANATION

A letter of rejection is prepared using an indirect style. Use personal letterhead with the proper date line, address of the recipient, and salutation. Your signature appears at the bottom beneath the complimentary close.

KEY POINTS

1. Use a buffer; start with a neutral opening that does not give a hint that the bad news is coming.

2. Provide reasons, explanation, or facts. Give the reasons why you cannot accept the job (not quite what I thought it would be; received another offer in an area that uses more of my preparation, etc.)

3. Tell the reader that, for the reasons just listed, you are sorry that you cannot accept the job.

4. Close in a pleasant way and include your thanks.

5. Proofread very carefully.

ACTIVITIES

1. Prepare a letter refusing a job offered to you.

2. Search the Internet for additional information about proper etiquette for refusing a job offer.

3. You were successful in your interviewing for an internship next semester; in fact, you were offered *two* internships. Write a letter *accepting* the one internship and a letter *rejecting* the other offer.

Kellie Seritt

1950 North Shore Drive • Port Hope, MI 48468 • (517) 555-5252 • kellieseritt@hotmail.com

May 31, 200x

Ms. Isadora Montez
Director of Marketing Research
The Montez Corporation
98765 South Boulder Street
Grand Forks, ND 54701

Dear Ms. Montez:

The interview I had with you last week was exciting and interesting. Your company is certainly on the cutting edge of the latest happenings in marketing research.

Your offering me the job was much appreciated; but, as I pointed out to you and the others who interviewed me, I am looking for a position that has a major emphasis in international sales. As a result, I am taking a job with Sellers Unlimited, where I will be the international director of sales.

Thank you so much for the interview and the job offer.

Sincerely,

Kellie Serritt

Kellie Seritt

| **TOPIC** | **Application follow-up letter** |

DEFINITION

An application follow-up letter is one sent to a company when you have not heard from that company and you want to know what happened to your application.

BACKGROUND

The application follow-up letter is written in direct style. You have not heard from the company, so you write a letter.
  a. Usually wait four to six weeks before you write the letter to give the company ample time to reply.
  b. Make the letter short and to the point. Tell the reader something new that you have done since you last wrote to the company.

KEY POINTS

1. Use block format; direct pattern.

2. Keep your letter brief.

3. Tell the reader something else you have done since you last talked to him or her.

4. Remind the reader that you want your application kept on file.

5. Proofread and edit the letter carefully.

ACTIVITIES

1. Write a letter to follow up an interview you had with a company several weeks ago. You have not heard from the company, and you want them to keep your application on file. Supply a name and address.

2. Check the Internet to see if you can find samples of application follow-up letters. How can you incorporate some of the information you found into your application follow-up letter?

3. Write a letter to follow up on an application you sent in several weeks ago. You have heard nothing from the company.

Nancy Kawalski
nekawak27@yahoo.com

7654 North Main Avenue
Grand Rapids, MI 49503

August 1, 200x

Mr. Roger McIntyre
Director of Personnel
McIntyre Products, Inc.
987 Oak Boulevard
Fargo, ND 58132

Dear Mr. McIntyre:

Since our last discussion about a month ago, I have completed a marketing research course at the local community college. In addition, I am now enrolled in the advanced marketing research class here at Central Michigan University.

Please keep my application active in your files. I am still interested in the position you have available, and I look forward to hearing from you soon.

Enclosed is an updated copy of my resume for your files.

Sincerely,

Nancy Kawalski

Nancy Kawalski

Enclosure

| **TOPIC** | **Letter of recommendation** |

DEFINITION

You may be asked to write a letter of recommendation by one of your friends or employees, or you may ask someone to write a letter of recommendation for you.

EXPLANATION

A letter of recommendation is usually written in the *direct* style because the letter should be a positive one. If you are asked to give a recommendation for someone and all you can say is unfavorable news, then do not give the recommendation.

KEY POINTS

Opening Paragraph

1. Name the applicant and the position sought.

2. Tell the reader that your remarks are confidential.

3. Describe your relationship with the candidate (fellow worker, former professor, former subordinate, etc.)

Body of the Letter

1. Describe the applicant's performance.

2. State what you think the applicant's potential is.

3. Include statements about organizational skills, people skills (does the applicant work well with people?) and communication skills.

4. Mention some of the tasks or projects the applicant has completed.

Closing

1. Summarize the candidate's strengths.

2. Rank the candidate. (Of all the marketing research people I have recommended, Maria ranks in the top 10 percent.)

3. Offer to supply additional information, if necessary. Provide a phone number or email address where applicant can ask for more information, if needed.

ACTIVITIES

1. Sometimes when you ask someone to write a letter of recommendation, he or she may say something like "Go ahead and write the letter for me; then I'll read and sign it." So, write a letter recommending yourself to an employer who is looking for someone with your skills and abilities.

2. Check out the Internet for examples of letters of recommendation and suggestions for writing a letter of recommendation. Prepare a short memo on suggestions for writing the recommendation letter, and read the memo to your classmates for comments and suggestions.

3. Write a recommendation letter for a co-worker and good friend of yours for a position with another company. The position is a step up from the one the person currently holds. Supply a name and address of the recipient. Assume any facts you need to complete the recommendation letter.

4. Your college roommate has asked you to write a letter of recommendation for an internship that is available during the summer. Assume any facts and information you wish, and write a letter of recommendation for your roommate. Supply a name and address of the recipient.

Dr. Robert T. Allison, Associate Professor   allis2rt@cmich.edu
Central Michigan University, Mount Pleasant, MI 48859   **(989) 774-4000**

May 29, 200x

Ms. Rosa Portales, Sales Director
Portales Enterprises, Inc.
12345 Main Avenue
Mount Pleasant, MI 48858

Dear Ms. Portales:

At the request of Sandra Simon, I submit to you a confidential letter of recommendation to support her application for the position of Assistant Sales Director at Portales. Ms. Simon was a student in my business communications class at Central Michigan University during the 200x-200x academic year.

Sandra's outstanding performance in my classroom is a strong indication of her work ethic on the job. Many students who have excelled in my class have succeeded well beyond my expectations in their current career. Not only was Sandra well organized and well prepared for every class, but she also communicated her thoughts and opinions in an efficient and effective manner. Every project and task that was handed out was completed on time and done with great detail to directions.

Sandra is a diligent worker as well as an intelligent and respectful person. Of all the students I have taught over the years, Sandra ranks among the top 5 percent. If you need additional information, please call me at (989) 774-4000.

Sincerely,

Robert T. Allison

Robert T. Allison
Associate Professor

TOPIC Interviewing

EXPLANATION Interviews are typically conducted in two ways—structured or unstructured.

1. Structured interviews consist of the same questions asked in the same sequence of each interviewee.

2. Unstructured interviews are informal and questions can vary from one applicant to another.

3. Trained recruiters structure interviews in three sections:
   a. Establishing cordial relationship
   b. Eliciting information from you
   c. Providing information about the job and company

KEY POINTS

1. Preparation for an interview is the key to a successful interview.
   a. The more you prepare, the more poised and confident you will be during the interview.

2. Prepare for an interview by researching the company.
   a. Learn about their history, check out their web site, find out what their unique strengths are, review their most recent annual report, read their mission statement, find out who their competitors are, check out their stock prices/market share, know about their products and services, know how many employees they have, and any recent news events.

3. Prepare for the interview with success stories.
   a. Put together a list of your skills, abilities, knowledge, and traits – focus on things that will set you apart from others.
   b. Target the skills employers' value most by reviewing the list of these skills on page 35.
   c. Avoid the common interview mistakes by reviewing the list on page 36.

4. Prepare for the interview by practicing your answers to common interview questions (see the "common interview questions" on pages 43-49).

5. Prepare your own questions to ask the interviewer regarding the position, the company, when the hiring decision is made, what the salary range is if not already discussed.

6. Take extra copies of your resume and your list of references with you to the interview.

7. Dress professionally (be conservative) and appropriately for the given industry; the interviewer will form an opinion of you based on your appearance within the first few seconds.

8. Arrive 10-15 minutes early.

9. Be on your best behavior before, during, and after the interview (you may be observed in the parking lot or the reception area).
    a. People begin forming negative or positive feelings toward you within the first 30 to 60 seconds of meeting you for the first time.

10. Practice your introduction for when you meet your interviewer(s).
    a. Be sure to stand up.
    b. Use a firm but painless handshake with only one or two "pumps" that lasts about 3 seconds.
    c. Make eye contact and smile.
    d. Introduce yourself with a greeting (*e.g.,* good morning).

11. Use a firm handshake, smile, and make eye contact when introducing yourself and when the interview concludes.
    a. People react positively to a firm handshake, direct eye contact, using their name, smiling, leaning forward when listening or talking, and projecting a firm pleasing tone of voice.

12. Expect to do about 50 percent of the talking during the interview.

13. The only item you should have available during an interview is a portfolio of some type that contains your resume and paper on which to take notes.

14. Pause to organize your thoughts before answering an open-ended question.

http://www.virginia.edu/career/students/job_search.html - provides information on preparing for the interview and helpful handouts.

www.job-interview.net - provides a complete interview guide plus interview questions and answers.

http://interview.monster.com/archives/attheinterview/ - provides lots of information for all aspects of the interview, including fashion mistakes, how hobbies can help you, response strategies, keeping your cool, curve-ball questions, the ten interview errors, questions they shouldn't ask, phone interviews, and interviewers' pet peeves.

What skills or abilities do employers value most in employees?

A survey of hundreds of recruiting professionals is conducted each year by the National Association of Colleges and Employers (NACE) to determine what kinds of major companies will be hiring for entry-level positions and what skills or abilities they're looking for in candidates.

The following is a list of the 11 most desirable skills and abilities:

1. Oral communication skills

2. Interpersonal skills

3. Analytical skills

4. Teamwork skills

5. Flexibility

6. Computer skills

7. Proficiency in field of study

8. Written communication skills

9. Leadership skills

10. Work experience

11. Internship or cooperative education experience

Another list of what top skills employers look for consists of the following skills:

1. Communication skills
2. Computer literacy
3. Flexibility
4. Team player
5. Self-motivation

Six Interview Mistakes
Written by Monster Contributing Writer Michael Neece

Avoid the typical interview traps by understanding the purpose and expectations of an interview. Here are six common interview traps to watch out for.

1. **Confusing an interview with an interrogation.**

    An interview is not an interrogation. Don't confuse the two! In an interrogation, only one person asks the questions and the other gives the answers. An interview is a business conversation where both people ask and answer questions. If you expect to be interrogated and don't ask any questions, you'll leave the interviewer in the reluctant role of interrogator.

2. **Making a so-called weakness seem positive.**

    On of the most common interview questions is "what are your weaknesses?" Conventional interview wisdom advises you to highlight a weakness like "I'm a perfectionist," and turn it into a positive. Interviewers aren't always impressed because they've heard this answer many times. The better approach to this question is to highlight a skill you wish to improve upon and describe what you are doing to enhance this skill. Interviewers don't care what your weaknesses are, they want to see how you handle the question and what your answer indicates about you.

3. **Failing to ask questions.**

    Every interview concludes with the interviewer asking if you have any questions. The worst thing to say is that you don't have any! This indicates you are not interested and are not prepared. Interviewers are more impressed by the questions you ask than the selling points you try to make. Make a list of questions <u>you</u> want to ask at the interview ahead of time.

4. **Researching the company but not yourself.**

    Candidates intellectually prepare by researching the company. Most candidates don't do the same preparation in researching themselves and taking inventory of their skills, experience, and knowledge. Formulate a talent inventory and write down an example from your life that demonstrates each. Remember to include technical skills, software applications, and discipline specific tools.

5. **Leaving your cell phone on.**

    A ringing cell phone is not appropriate for an interview. Turn it off (don't leave it on and set it to vibrate) before you enter the building. Better yet, don't even take it with you.

6. **Waiting for a call.**

    Time is your enemy after the interview. After you send a thank-you email and note to every interviewer, follow up a couple days later with either a question or additional information. Contact the person who can hire you and not the HR department. HR is famous for not returning calls. You goal is to keep everyone's memory of you fresh.

TOPIC **Meal interview (and dining etiquette)**

EXPLANATION Interviews over lunch or dinner are gaining in popularity. If part of your interview involves dining out, be sure to review proper dining etiquette beforehand (resources are given on page 38 also). You need to pay attention to how look while eating and know proper table manners.

KEY POINTS

1. No personal items should be on the table when dining; no keys, no purses, no folders.
2. Be aware – no elbows on the table, don't chew with your mouth open or talk with food in your mouth.
3. Be polite – say please and thank you to everyone, including the wait staff.
4. Brush up on table manners before the interview to be prepared and confident.
5. Order carefully – follow the lead from your interviewer and order something in the same price range and the same number of courses. Avoid messy or difficult foods to eat. Order foods that are easy to eat with a knife and fork.
6. Talk and eat – wait for everyone at the table to be served before you begin eating. Not eating can indicate nervousness, so answer questions and ask them to give yourself the chance to eat.
7. Ending the meal – it is never appropriate to ask for a doggy bag in this situation. Don't offer to pay. Reaffirm your interest to the interviewer combined with a handshake and "thank you." Follow up with a thank-you letter or email the next day.

ACTIVITIES

1. Do research on business etiquette to learn more about proper business etiquette as it relates to all aspects of job hunting. Check out business etiquette practices for any country, including the U.S., at http://executiveplanet.com/.

2. Do you know about proper job-hunting etiquette? Take the online etiquette quiz at http://quintcareers.com/job-hunting_etiquette_quiz.html to test your knowledge on a variety of business etiquette areas. Test your etiquette further, including dining etiquette with the quiz at www.amlgroup.com/quiz.html.

Dining Etiquette:
http://www.bsu.edu/students/careers/students/interviewing/dining/

Table manners:
http://www.bsu.edu/students/careers/students/interviewing/dinetips/

International business culture and etiquette:
www.executiveplanet.com/

TOPIC   **Telephone interview**

EXPLANATION   Many companies use telephone interviews as a screening technique as well as to save time and money. This type of interview is typically brief (20-30 minutes) with one or more people. Phone interviews can be challenging because you have no visual connection to your interviewer(s). With no nonverbal cues and body language it's difficult to gauge your performance. If you're invited for a face-to-face interview, you know you succeeded.

Prepare for a phone interview the same way as you would any other interview, but with a few additions and modifications explained below.

KEY POINTS

1. Treat the phone interview as seriously you would for an in-person interview. Don't be casual or informal. Research the company and prepare your responses. Stand up or sit up straight at a table or desk to improve your psychological frame of mind.

2. Have your resume, cover letter, and the job posting in front of you. Bring any other notes that will help you remember any key points, skills, or experiences you want to be sure to mention.

3. Use a high-quality phone. Cell phones do not always have the best quality reception or dependability.

4. Arrange for complete privacy and ensure there will be no interruptions during the interview.

ACTIVITIES

1. Select <u>one</u> of the lists of common interview questions on pages 43-49 and outline your answers to each question to include in your employment resource portfolio (part of the Capstone Project for this unit).

2. Read about the "six interview mistakes" on page 36. Prepare five questions you would ask at a job interview to avoid making mistake #3 on the list. Then prepare your "talent inventory" outlining your experience, skills, and knowledge to avoid making mistake #4.

3. Go to the Job-Interview.net web site at www.job-interview.net/. Click on "mock job interviews" and follow the instructions to complete a mock interview based on specific career fields, actual job openings, and job description. Each mock interview includes a practice question set, answer tips, and interview resources. This web site also provides great interview tips, answers to 900+ possible interview questions, and questions to ask the interviewer.

4. Searching for information about a company is in some ways a treasure hunt. After you have narrowed your job search down to one or two companies, you may wish to do a thorough investigation of the company. Some prospective employees complete a research of the company before they have narrowed down the companies for whom they want to work. Either way you do it, researching a company will provide you with excellent information about the company.

At the end of this activity is a list of company directories, both national and international that will aid you in your job search. Here are some of the items you will want to investigate. Perhaps you will find other items not listed here that will be helpful to you in your investigation.

   a. Name of the company.
   b. Short history and background of the company.
   c. Location of home office, president's name, and number or employees.
   d. Branch offices.
   e. Ranking of company from the *Fortune* list.
   f. The current price and the high and low range of the company stock for this year (assuming the company is listed on a stock exchange).
   g. The current P/E ratio.
   h. A company brochure or a company fact sheet. What is included in the brochure or fact sheet?
   i. What is the latest business plan?

4. Write a job description for which you could apply. Items to be included in a job description may include the following:

   a. Job title
   b. Job responsibilities and duties
   c. Degree required
   d. Skills involved
   e. Working environment
   f. Salary

5. This assignment incorporates the use of the Internet, a trip or two to the library, and perhaps even a call or letter to the company itself. Some students in the past have been invited in to talk to one of the officers. Companies like the idea of helping students complete a project because the company image is being promoted at the same time.

   Prepare the report under the direction of your instructor, who will suggest a proper format for presenting your data.

   Company Directories

   Directory of Corporate Affiliations. (Annual.) Providence, NJ: National Register Publishing.

   Million Dollar Directory: America's Leading Public & Private Companies (Annual.) Parsippany, NJ: Dun and Bradstreet.

   Moody's Manuals. (Annual, with semiweekly supplements). New York: Moody's Investors Service.

   Standard and Poor's Register of Corporations, Directors and Executives. (Annual.) New York: Standard and Poor's.

   Ward's Business Directory of U.S. Private and Public Companies. (Annual.) Detroit: Gale Research.

   World Business Directory. Detroit: Gale Research.

6. Study four of the company directories listed in #5 above. Compare each of the four as to what type of information they contain and how these sources can be helpful to you in your job search. Submit a memo of your comparisons to your instructor.

7. How well do you know yourself? How well do you understand yourself? Self-evaluation can help you determine what you are looking for in a job. Below are several questions that should provide you with a look at what you are really after in terms of a job. Recruiters may ask you some of these questions, but the purpose of this exercise is to get to know what you really want in a job.

   Write out answers to the following questions. Then in a few months, write out the answers to the following questions again. See if your expectations have changed. Here are the questions:

a. Would I work better in a large or a small organization?
b. How important is geographic location to me? To my family?
c. Do I work better alone or as a member of a group?
d. Am I a follower or a leader?
e. Do I think before I act?
f. Do I like working with people or with things?
g. Do I work well under pressure?
h. Do I have good ideas?
i. Do I listen well?
j. Do I make proper decisions?
k. Do I express myself well in writing and orally?
l. What do I admire in others?
m. What do I enjoy doing most?
n. What accomplishments have satisfied me most?
o. What are my shortcomings? What have I done to correct my shortcomings?
p. What do I want to be doing five years from now? Ten years from now?
q. What skills and knowledge do I need to achieve my five- and ten-year goals?

RESOURCES

http://www.seekingsuccess.com/articles/art167.php3 - an article on telephone interviews; includes a "quick tips" list.

http://www.worktree.com/tb/IN_telephone.cfm - an article on mastering the telephone interview; includes other employment-related resources as well.

http://www.assignmentsplus.com/telephone-interview.html - provides great tips on preparing for a telephone interview.

TOP TEN INTERVIEW QUESTIONS

Preparing for an interview is important. According to Carole Martin, Monster.com contributing writer, too many job seekers stumble through interviews as if the questions are coming out of left field. But many interview questions can be expected! Study this list of the top ten interview questions and plan your answers before the interview so you can deliver them with confidence. Use the tips provided for each question in formulating your answers.

1. **What are your weaknesses?**

   This is the most dreaded question of all. Handle it by <u>minimizing your weakness</u> and emphasizing your strengths. *Stay away from personal qualities and concentrate on professional traits:* "I am always working on improving my communication skills to be a more effective presenter. I recently joined Toastmasters, which I find very helpful."

2. **Why should we hire you?**

   <u>Summarize your experiences</u>: "With five years' experience working in the financial industry and my proven record of saving the company money, I could make a big difference in your company. I'm confident I would be a great addition to your team."

3. **Why do you want to work here?**

   The interviewer is listening for an <u>answer</u> that indicates you've given this some thought and are not sending out resumes just because there is an opening. For example, "I've selected key companies whose mission statements are in line with my values, where I know I could be excited about what the company does, and this company is very high on my list of desirable choices."

4. **What are your goals?**

   Sometimes it's best to talk about <u>short-term and intermediate goals</u> rather than locking yourself into the distant future. For example, "My immediate goal is to get a job in a growth-oriented company. My long-term goal will depend on where the company goes. I hope to eventually grow into a position of responsibility."

5. **Why did you leave (or why are you leaving) your job?**

   If you're unemployed, state your reason for leaving in a positive context: "I managed to survive two rounds of corporate downsizing, but the third round was a 20 percent reduction in the workforce, which included me."

   If you are employed, focus on what you want in your next job: "After two years, I made the decision to look for a company that is team-focused, where I can add my experience."

6. **When were you most satisfied in your job?**

   The interviewer wants to know what <u>motivates you</u>. If you can relate an example of a job or project when you were excited, the interviewer will get an idea of your preferences. "I was very satisfied in my last job because I worked directly with the customers and their problems; that is an important part of the job for me."

preferences. "I was very satisfied in my last job because I worked directly with the customers and their problems; that is an important part of the job for me."

7. What can you do for us that other candidates can't?
What makes you unique? This will take an assessment of your experiences, skills, and traits. Summarize concisely: "I have a unique combination of strong technical skills, and the ability to build strong customer relationships. This allows me to use my knowledge and break down information to be more user-friendly."

8. What are three positive things your last boss would say about you?
It's time to pull out your old performance appraisals and boss's quotes. This is a great way to brag about yourself through someone else's words: "My boss has told me that I am the best designer he has ever had. He knows he can rely on me, and he likes my sense of humor."

9. What salary are you seeking?
It is to your advantage if the employer tells you the range first. <u>Prepare</u> by knowing the going rate in your area, and your bottom line or walk-away point. One possible answer would be: "I am sure when the time comes, we can agree on a reasonable amount. In what range do you typically pay someone with my background?"

10. If you were an animal, which one would you want to be?
Interviewers use this type of psychological question to see if you can think quickly. If you answer "a bunny," you will make a soft, passive impression. If you answer "a lion," you will be seen as aggressive. What type of personality would it take to get the job done? What impression do you want to make?

MOST COMMON INTERVIEW QUESTIONS

LIST 1

The following lists of interview questions are considered some of the most commonly asked interview questions. Read through the following lists; you'll notice some similarities.

1. Why do you want to work for us?

2. Why should we hire you?

3. What can you tell me about yourself?

4. What are your strongest (or weakest) personal qualities?

5. What do you expect to be doing in ten years?

6. Do you prefer working with others or by yourself?

7. Have you ever changed your major during your education? Why?

8. What have been your most rewarding or disappointing work (or school) experiences?

9. Have you established any new goals lately?

10. What are your long- and short-term goals?

11. What were your best and worst subjects in college?

12. What sort of jobs did you have while you were in college?

13. What makes you happiest at work?

MOST COMMON INTERVIEW QUESTIONS
LIST 2:

1. Tell me about yourself.

2. What do you know about our company?

3. Why do you want to work for us?

4. What unique qualities or abilities would you bring this job?

5. What are your major strengths and weaknesses?

6. How long do you plan to stay at our company?

7. Where do you see yourself in five years?

8. Tell me about a time that you failed at something, and what you did afterwards.

9. What do you do in your spare time?

10. Describe a time when you worked on a team project. What was your relative position on the team? Were you satisfied with your contribution? How could it have been better?

11. Why did you choose your school and course of study?

12. Think back to a situation in which a conflict existed. Tell me how you resolved that conflict.

13. Tell me about a project that you completed. Describe in detail how you managed it and describe the outcome.

14. What salary are you expecting?

15. What other types of jobs or companies are you considering?

MOST COMMON INTERVIEW QUESTIONS

LIST 3:

1. Describe the characteristics of an individual whom you especially admire.

2. What is important to you in a job?

3. What do you think determines a person's progress in an organization?

4. Describe something you've done that shows initiative and willingness to work.

5. Describe a time when you worked well under pressure.

6. Describe a time when you worked effectively with others.

7. Describe a time when you organized a major project.

8. Describe a time when you motivated and led others.

9. Describe a time when you solved a difficult problem.

10. Describe a time when you accepted constructive criticism.

11. What position do you plan to have in five years?

12. What are your greatest strengths?

13. When did you choose your college major and what are some of the factors that led you to choose your major?

14. What are some of the factors that led you to choose the university you attended?

MOST COMMON INTERVIEW QUESTIONS

LIST 4:

1. Tell us about yourself.

2. What are your career plans (long term and short term)? What position do you plan to have in five years?

3. What are some of the factors that led you to choose your college major? Your college/university? When did you choose your college major?

4. What courses did you like least? Best? Explain.

5. What do you know about opportunities in the field in which you are trained?

6. What do you know about our company? Why do you want to work for us?

7. Why should we hire you? What qualifications do you have that make you feel that you should be hired over others?

8. What do you consider your greatest strengths and/or weaknesses?

9. What do you think determines a person's progress in an organization?

10. How do your qualifications compare with the job requirements?

11. Describe a time when you (a) worked well under pressure, (b) worked effectively with others, (c) organized a major project, (d) motivated and led others, (e) solved a difficult problem, and (f) accepted constructive criticism.

12. Describe something you have done that shows initiative and willingness to work.

13. How have your extracurricular activities, part-time work experience, or volunteer work prepared you for work in our company?

14. What is important to you in a job? What interests you most about this job?

15. What are your salary expectations?

16. Describe the characteristics of an individual whom you especially admire.

17. Are you willing to take some psychological or drug tests?

SELECTED BEHAVIORAL INTERVIEW QUESTIONS

LIST 5:

Behavioral interview questions are ones that make you think through a situation and give a careful, well-planned answer to the question. Here are a few examples of behavioral interview questions that you may wish to practice before your interview:

1. How have you demonstrated initiative in the past six months?

2. Think about a difficult boss, professor, or other person. What made him or her difficult? How did you successfully interact with this person?

3. Think about a complex project or assignment you have been given. What approach did you take to complete the project or assignment?

4. Tell me about an occasion where you needed to work with a group to get a job done.

5. Tell me about a time when you worked with a person who did things very differently from you. How did you get the job done?

6. Describe your two or three greatest accomplishments to date.

7. Tell me about a challenge that you successfully met.

8. What leadership positions have you held? Describe your leadership style.

9. Summarize a situation where you successfully persuaded others to do something or to see your point of view.

10. What new ideas or suggestions have you generated while at school or work?

11. Describe a situation where class assignments and work or personal activities conflicted. How did you prioritize? How did you manage your time? What was the outcome?

12. Tell me about a complex problem you solved. Describe the process you used.

According to a human resources professional for one of Michigan's largest employers, the following questions are asked of all interviewees at this company:

1. With what teamwork activities have you been involved?

2. How did you deal with confrontation with this team?

3. How did you facilitate change and deal with others in the group who had a different point of view or opinion than you?

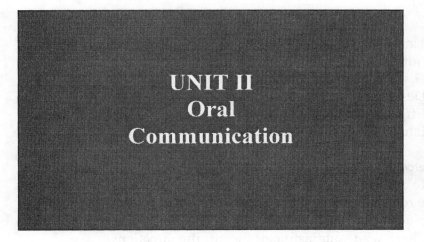

UNIT II
Oral
Communication

The Capstone Project for Unit II is designed to apply the main topics in this unit into one integrated activity. You will experience each step of preparing and giving an oral presentation, including a self-assessment component. The integration of the unit topics via the completion of these activities will increase your understanding of effective communication, including interpersonal communication within a team setting while improving your oral communication skills. This assignment will consist of the following elements:

1. Prepare an outline of an oral presentation to inform (3-5 minutes in length is recommended) following the "golden rule of public speaking" as explained in this unit.

2. Complete a *related factors report* (based on the four related factors explained on page 59).

3. Design an effective visual aid designed to use in your oral presentation.

4. Prepare a videotape of yourself giving your oral presentation.

5. Complete *video feedback self-evaluation* (self-evaluation questions provided on page 66).

Instructions for Capstone Project:

1. Form teams of 3-5 students and compile a *team oral communication resource file* that includes resources and information on the following topics:
   a. Giving effective presentations
   b. Designing effective visual aids
   c. Effective teams and teambuilding issues
   d. Intercultural communications

2. When you have completed your *team oral communication resource file*, each team will give a 10-15 minute oral presentation to inform based on your findings. Your purpose is to inform the rest of the class about the resources and information your team found for each topic or your instructor may assign one topic per team to give their presentation on. Check with your instructor for specific directions.

3. Prepare an outline of your team presentation (follow the "golden rule") and design appropriate visual aids.

4. Utilize all the topics in Unit II to complete this activity.

Note: Evaluation forms are included in the *Appendix* of this text for evaluating an oral report to inform (instructor and peer evaluations), team presentation evaluation forms (instructor and peer evaluations), and an audience evaluation form, pages 199-204..

TOPIC	**Communication process**

DEFINITION

Three key elements of the communication process are the following:
1. verbal communication
2. nonverbal communication
3. listening

1. **Verbal communication** consists of the spoken words we use to communicate, including the way we speak, such as voice level, phrasing, rate of speech, and volume. Consider these tips from Toastmasters International (www.toastmasters.org):
   a. know the room
   b. know the audience
   c. know your material
   d. relax
   e. visualize yourself giving your speech
   f. realize that people want you to succeed
   g. do not apologize
   h. concentrate on the message—not the medium
   i. turn nervousness into positive energy
   j. gain experience

2. **Nonverbal communication** consists of the unspoken signs we communicate with through our body language, facial expressions, eye contact, appearance, space, and time. This form of communication is often ambiguous since interpretation of these attributes can vary greatly between individuals, genders, and cultures. To improve nonverbal communication skills, apply the following items:
   a. maintain eye contact with the listener (see special section on improving your eye communication on page 55).
   b. reduce or eliminate physical barriers
   c. probe for more information
   d. be wary of assigning nonverbal meanings out of context
   e. associate with people from diverse cultures
   f. observe yourself on video tape occasionally

3. **Listening** is a conscious process to hear sounds. Most people are very inefficient listeners due to a variety of barriers to listening that constantly challenge our focus. Numerous mental and physical barriers distract and compete for our attention and prevent us from listening effectively, such as noise, our state of mind, the time of day, and much more. Apply the items from the following checklist for improving your listening:

a. Talk less; listen more. Concentrate on what the speaker is saying.
b. Block out distracting thoughts.
c. Turn off the TV; shut the window; remove all distractions.
d. Be tolerant of all speakers.
e. Paraphrase the speaker's ideas by silently repeating the message; summarize the ideas in your own words silently.
f. Observe nonverbal cues. What is the speaker really saying?

KEY POINTS

1. Improving our communication skills requires improving each of the three key elements of the communication process.

2. Research shows that when verbal and nonverbal cues conflict, people will determine meaning from the nonverbal cues.
   - 55 percent of the first impact you have is nonverbal; 33 percent is the way you use your voice, and 12 percent is the actual words you say.

3. Meanings of nonverbal communication are determined by and can vary between the different cultural group(s) you belong to.
   a. Assigned meanings can vary greatly between different individuals and groups.
   b. You may belong to multiple cultural groups of various sizes through membership in an ethnic group, your family, your profession, your social group, and other groups.

4. Nonverbal communication is multi-sensory (see, smell, feel, taste, and hear).

5. Be aware of the barriers that make it difficult for you to listen effectively and efficiently (mental and physical barriers).
   - Learn to improve your focus for better listening by eliminating or learning to ignore barriers.

6. The average person listens very inefficiently, not hearing and processing as much as 75 percent of what is spoken.
   a. The best communicators are excellent listeners.
   b. Practice is necessary to be an efficient listener.

7. Improving your eye communication
    a. Your eyes are the only part of your central nervous system that directly connect with another person. In the business world, you use your eyes to communicate 90 percent of the time in face-to-face conversations.

8. Remember the three "I's" of eye communication: (a) intimacy; (b) intimidation; and (3) involvement.

    a. *intimacy* and *intimidation* involve looking at a person from 10 seconds to a minute or more.

    b. *involvement* is what is called for in almost every personal communication, especially in a business setting.
        1.) Involvement means looking at someone for 5-10 seconds before looking away. This is natural for one-on-one communication, but is also what should be practiced whether speaking to one person or a room full of people.

Eye communication tips:
➢ Avoid darting eyes (what we tend to do when we're nervous).
➢ Darting eyes undermine your credibility.
➢ Look directly at a person and hold eye contact for a few seconds at a time.
➢ You can develop the five second habit with practice.
➢ Observe how others use eye contact and notice what makes you feel comfortable and uncomfortable.

ACTIVITIES

1. Test your nonverbal communication skills with this activity: first, find someone in your class whose birthday is the same month as yours <u>without</u> speaking; second, find someone in your class who has the same color car as yours <u>without</u> speaking.

    a. Find additional information and resources on nonverbal communication at this Ohio State library site: www.lib.ohio-state.edu/gateway/bib/nonverbal.html

2. Test your listening skills by playing the grapevine game. One person starts by whispering a short message (1-2 sentences) into another person's ear.

    a. The second person then passes the message on to the third person, then to the fourth person, and so on.

b. When the last person receives the message he or she tells the entire class what the message was they heard to the entire class and the first person tells what the message was originally.

c. Compare the messages… how good were your listening skills?

3. Find a journal article that discusses ways you can improve your listening skills. Prepare a one-page summary of the article.

4. Find a journal article that discusses ways you can improve your nonverbal communication skills.

a. Prepare a one-page summary of the article according to your instructor's direction.

5. Form teams of 3-5 students, then brainstorm as a team to list all the barriers you can think of that prevent us from being good listeners.

a. Categorize your list of barriers as either *mental* or *physical*.

b. Discuss what the most common barriers are for each team member and identify ways you can eliminate or learn to ignore these barriers.

c. When completed with your team's list, check your list against the list of common communication barriers provided at www.nsba.org/sbot/toolkit/CommStyl.html

RESOURCES

Communication process:

http://ollie.dcccd.edu/mgmt1374/book_contents/3organizing/commun/communic.htm - an explanation of the communication process, with illustrations of the components.

http://teampublish.allsoldout.net/teampubv3/includes/Ombcur5.pdf - a thorough explanation on all aspects of the communication process (in .pdf file format).

Listening:

http://www.d.umn.edu/student/loon/acad/strat/ss_listening.html - provides strategies for improving your listening skills.

http://www.positive-way.com/listenin.htm - complete an online evaluation of your listening skills; provides advice on improving your listening skills.

http://www.csbsju.edu/academicadvising/help/eff-list.html - provides a list of basics for effective listening and note taking.

Nonverbal communication:

http://www3.usal.es/~nonverbal/introduction.htm - provides a list of links to resources related to nonverbal communication including links to researchers web sites, papers, abstracts, and journals on this topic.

http://honolulu.hawaii.edu/intranet/committees/FacDevCom/guidebk/teach tip/commun-1.htm - article on "six ways to improve your nonverbal communication."

http://www.mhhe.com/socscience/speech/commcentral/mgnonverbal.html - information on all aspects of nonverbal communication.

Verbal communication:

http://www.itstime.com/aug97.htm - an online newsletter targeting the improvement of verbal communication and all aspects of communication.

http://www.queendom.com/cgi-bin/tests/transfer.cgi - complete an online communication skills test

Communication skills:

http://www.brianmac.demon.co.uk/commun.htm - information on communication skills and the various factors related to effective communication; includes links to related web sites and journals.

http://www.brianmac.demon.co.uk/commun.htm - tips on improving your communication skills; includes links to articles on introductory communication skills, better public speaking, speaking to an audience, communicating in your organization, communicating internationally, win-win negotiation, and other related topics.

Oral presentations

1. Communication skills are consistently ranked as the skills most valued in the business world.

2. Communication skills are consistently ranked as the #1 skill for success by top executives, both male and female.

3. Effective presentations are well planned, well organized, and delivered well.

4. Your most important tool for an effective presentation is an outline that enables you to plan, organize, and deliver effectively.

5. Your outline should follow the "golden rule" of public speaking (see template page 64 and example outline page 65):
   a. Tell them what you're going to say
   b. Say it
   c. Tell them what you said

6. There are three basic types of oral presentations:
   a. Informative
   b. Persuasive
   c. Entertaining

7. The most important factor to increase the success of an oral presentation is <u>practice</u>.
   a. The only way to improve your skills is to gain experience by giving oral presentations.
   b. A major obstacle in improving presentation skills is the lack of awareness of how bad you really are.

8. Speak from an outline that follows the "golden rule" of oral presentations.
   a. Print your outline on standard sized paper (no index cards).
   b. Use a larger font size if it helps you to better follow your outline when speaking.

9. Do not forget the impact of nonverbal communication on your oral presentation.
   a. Nonverbal communication can enhance or detract from your presentation.
   b. Effective use of eye contact makes you appear credible and confident to your audience.

1. Identify the topic and purpose (to inform, persuade, or entertain) of your oral presentation.

2. Research your topic as necessary.

3. Check out each of the *related factors* that directly affect your presentation:
    a. <u>Time factor</u> – first, you must find out the amount of time you're expected to speak before you can prepare your presentation.

    b. <u>Audience factor</u> – know the makeup of your audience; the audience is crucial in determining the tone of your presentation and in determining the appropriate level of vocabulary and technical terms.

    c. <u>Room factor</u> – know the size of the room you'll be speaking in, the type of seating and room arrangement, the speaker's platform or podium arrangement, and be familiar with any technical equipment you'll be using (microphone, computer, remote control).

    d. <u>Scheduling factor</u> – find out what time of the day you are speaking and the placement of your presentation among other presenters; these factors make a difference in audience mood, ability to focus, attention span, and other factors.

4. Outline your presentation following the "golden rule" of oral presentations – (see example outline on page 64).
    a. Outline the "introduction" including an attention getter and introduction of your main points.

    b. Outline the "body" of your presentation by outlining each of your major points, providing adequate support for each.

    c. Outline the "summary" of your presentation by re-stating your main points and if appropriate, asking for questions.

5. Prepare at least one visual aid that <u>enhances</u> your presentation as outlined in the "Guidelines for Visual Aids" topic beginning on page 67.

6. Remember the two "P's" of effective presentations: *preparation* and *practice.*

7. Confidence is the key to effective public speaking and can only be gained through thorough preparation and practice.
   a. Practicing your presentation is the only way to make sure you are within the time frame allotted.
   b. Practicing your presentation is the only way to be comfortable with your material, visual aids, and equipment.

ACTIVITIES

1. Impromptu speaking activity—everyone needs to bring an item in a paper bag to class without telling anyone what your item is.

   a. Optional – conduct peer evaluations as part of this activity by having three students evaluate each speaker (a peer evaluation form is included in the *Appendix)..*

   b. All students place their bagged item on a table when they come into class.

   c. Everyone will take a turn selecting a bag from the table, seeing what is in it, and giving a two-minute oral presentation to inform.

   d. The "on-deck" student can step out in the hall after selecting the bag to prepare for the oral presentation while another student is giving his or her presentation; this procedure allows each student about two minutes to prepare.

   e. Remember to follow the "golden rule" of oral presentations and you will be able to give a much more organized and effective presentation. *Hint*: Start with an introduction of yourself, your topic (whatever your item is) and some kind of attention getter; then pick two to three major points you want to discuss about the item, *e.g.,* three uses of the item); then conclude by re-stating your major points!

2. Prepare an outline following the "golden rule" based on a topic you choose for a three-minute oral presentation to inform (part of the Capstone Project for this unit).

3. Check out the *related* factors (as explained in this topic on page 59 and listed below) that will affect your oral presentation to inform as assigned in *Activity 2* above (part of the Capstone Project for this unit).

    a. Prepare your *report of related factors* for the four related factors listed below.

    b. Discuss the implications of each factor and how each factor affects your planning, preparation, and presentation:
        1) Time factor
        2) Audience factor
        3) Room factor
        4) Scheduling factor

4. Videotape yourself giving an oral presentation according to your instructor's directions (part of the Capstone Project for this unit).

    a. Prepare your *video feedback self-evaluation* by viewing your videotaped oral presentation and answering the questions on page 66 (part of the Capstone Project for this unit).

    b. Refer to the following *elements of effective oral presentations checklist* on page 63 to help you complete this activity.

    c. Check with your instructor for format requirements and any other instructions for completing this activity.

5. Meet with your teammates to begin compiling your *team oral communication resource file* (part of the Capstone Project for this unit).

    a. Visit web sites that provide information on giving effective presentations and printout information from these web sites to include in your team's resource file.

1. 3M Meeting Network web site provides information on creating and delivering effective presentations, as well as how to run effective meetings; in addition, you can download unique presentation templates: www.3m.com/meetingnetwork

2. Effective Presentations web site designed to provide many links, resources, and online tutorials for the improvement of oral presentation skills: www.kumc.edu/SAH/OTEd/jradel/effective.html

3. Presentation Helper web site for designing effective visual presentations, includes "the seven deadly sins of visual presentations": www.presentationhelper.co.uk/7sinsvisual.htm

4. Presenters University web site includes information on delivery and visual aids with tutorials: www.presentersuniversity.com/visuals.php

5. Web site for Toastmasters International includes "10 Tips for Successful Public Speaking": www.toastmasters.org/tips.asp

6. Reference web site for planning effective presentations: www.startwright.com/presenta.htm

7. Small Business: Canada web site offers business tips on "giving effective PowerPoint presentations": http://sbinfocanada.about.com/library/biztips/bl_biztips_14.htm

8. Information on "creating an effective PowerPoint presentation: http://people.csp.edu/saylor/effective_powerpoint.htm

9. Web site for interpersonal communication information and resources, including links to information on interpersonal communications: www.gpsi.com/interper.html

10. Speakers Platform web site includes a library resource containing hundreds of valuable articles about public speaking and related issues by leading experts: www.speaking.com/articles.html

Elements of Effective Oral Presentations - Checklist

Note: The following is an example of an oral presentations checklist. Use this list or something similar when you prepare a presentation or when you listen to someone else giving a presentation.

_____ Effective use of eye contact

_____ Well prepared; meets time requirements

_____ Content is well organized, logical

_____ Effective use of visual aids

_____ Well-designed visual aids

_____ Uses appropriate volume and rate of speech

_____ Uses natural speaking voice

_____ Confident, relaxed appearance

_____ Uses effective phrasing and emphasis

_____ Avoids distracting gestures

_____ Uses proper tone and enthusiasm

Golden Rule for Oral Presentations

(1) Tell them what you're going to say

(2) Say it

(3) Tell them what you said

ORAL PRESENTATION OUTLINE TEMPLATE

Follow this format for planning and delivering a well-organized oral presentation that follows the "golden rule":

I. Introduction

A. *Introduce yourself*

B. *Include an attention getter*

C. *Introduce your topic*

> Good attention getters include asking a question or stating an impressive fact or startling statistic

1. *Preview your main points #1* (tell them what you're going to say)

2. *Main point #2*

3. *Main point #3*

II. Body (say it)

A. *Main point #1*

1. *Sub point (supporting information)*

2. *Sub point, etc.*

B. *Main point #2*

1. *Sub point (supporting information)*

2. *Sub point, etc.*

C. *Main point #3*

1. *Sub point (supporting information)*

2. *Sub point, etc.*

III. Summary

A. *Restate your main points* (tell them what you said).

B. Ask for questions if appropriate

TOPIC: The Amish Way of Life

PURPOSE: To inform

I.   Introduction
      A. Welcome and introduce myself
      B. Imagine life without TV
      C. Amish way of life
          1. Lifestyle
          2. Clothing
          3. Religion

Tell them what you're going to say (Introduction)

II.   Body
      A. Lifestyle
          1. No telephone
          2. No electricity
          3. Source of transportation
      B. Clothing
          1. Men's
              a. Buttons only
              b. Pants with suspenders
          2. Women's
              a. Dresses
              b. Black cape/bonnet
          3. Children's
              a. Girls
              b. Boys
      C. Religion
          1. Take turns with services
          2. Big meal
          3. Games

Say it (Body)

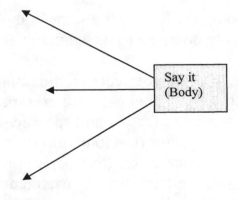

III.   Summary
      A. Lifestyle, clothing, religion
      B. Any questions?

Tell them what you said (Summary)

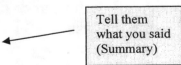

Video Feedback Self-Evaluation Instructions and Questions
For an Oral Presentation
(part of the capstone project for this unit)

1st – Watch your videotaped oral presentation in its entirety when you have no distractions.

2nd – Watch your videotaped presentation a second time; reflect on how you felt while you were giving your presentation (nervous, relaxed, etc.), and answer the following questions:

1. What do you feel you did best?

2. What do you feel needs the most improvement? What can you do to improve on this factor the next time?

3. How did your audience react/respond during your presentation and how did this response make you feel?

4. If you were to give the same oral presentation again, what changes would you make to the content?

5. How well do you feel you did in preparing for each of the "related factors" listed below? -Refer to page 59 as needed for explanations of each "related factor" and specific points to discuss.
   - Time factor (too long, too short, under prepared, etc.)
   - Audience factor (tone, appropriate vocabulary, etc.)
   - Room factor (seating arrangement, familiarity with equipment, podium, etc.)
   - Scheduling factor (prepared for mood of audience, barriers, etc.)

6. List <u>two</u> goals you have to further develop your oral presentation skills.

7. Rate your overall performance on a scale of 1-10 with "1" being lowest and "10" being highest.

Guidelines for visual aids

1. Visual aids can increase the persuasiveness of a presentation, the comprehension by audience members, and the perception of the credibility and professionalism of the presenter.

2. Well-designed visual aids enhance a presentation, making it more interesting and making the presenter appear better prepared by audience members.

3. A variety of visual aids may be used, such as:
   a. Objects, models
   b. Maps, graphs, charts
   c. Pictures (posters, photographs, drawings)
   d. Boards used to write on (chalkboard, whiteboard, flipcharts)
   e. Media items (films, video, audio recordings)
   f. Presentation technology (slides, transparencies)
   g. Handouts

4. Basic rules for designing effective visual aids relate to <u>four</u> key issues:
   a. **Visibility** – minimum font sizes to use for handouts, transparencies, and slides vary (see chart below).
   b. **Emphasis/content** – visual aids should compliment and enhance your presentation; do not try to put "everything" in your text-based visual aids; focus on relevance and simplicity in designing visual aids.
   c. **Balance** – visuals should be appealing to your audience with well-balanced use of text, color, graphics, etc.
   d. **Color** – use appropriate colors so that your text-based visuals are not difficult to read; make sure your audience can see and read your visuals easily.
      1) Check the background colors for ease of readability given the light and size of the room in which you will be presenting.
      2) Be sure the font size is large enough and the color distinct so as not to blend in with the background.

Text-Based Visual Aids - Recommended Font Sizes			
	Handouts	**Transparencies**	**Slide**
Title:	36 pt	24 pt	18 pt
Subtitles:	24 pt	18 pt	14 pt
Other text:	18 pt	14 pt	12 pt

5. Be sure to give visuals like slides and transparencies a test run in the room you will be presenting in or a similar environment to check for readability in the lighting your presentation will be viewed in and the room size.
   a. Will everyone be able to see and read your visuals, no matter where they are seated?

6. Be sure to practice your presentation with your visual aids and any equipment, controls, lights, etc.
   a. Do stand to the side of visual aids, never in front.
   b. Do use a pointing device if appropriate.
   c. Do not point at the screen when using transparencies or slides-- point at the transparency on the projector or point out something on a slide with the mouse or pointing device.

7. Know the placement of any visual aids within your presentation and be sure to refer your audience to the visual by page number, using a pointing device, or whatever is appropriate.
   a. Distribute any handouts before or after your presentation, not during.
   b. Do not display a visual until you need to refer to it.
   c. Point out where material you are discussing can be found if your audience has a handout (*i.e.,* page number).
   d. Do remove a visual as soon as you have covered it.

ACTIVITIES

1. Visit web sites that provide information on designing effective visuals to add to your team's *oral communication resource file* (part of the Capstone Project for this unit).

RESOURCES

1. Effective Presentations web site provides resources, links, and online tutorials for designing effective presentations: www.kumc.edu/SAH/OTEd/jradel/effective.html

2. Presentation Helper web site for designing effective visual presentations, includes "the seven deadly sins of visual presentations": www.presentationhelper.co.uk/7sinsvisual.htm

3. Presenters University web site includes information on delivery and visual aids with tutorials: www.presentersuniversity.com/visuals.php

4. Reference web site for planning effective presentations: www.startwright.com/presenta.htm

5. Small Business: Canada web site offers business tips on "giving effective PowerPoint presentations": http://sbinfocanada.about.com/library/biztips/bl_biztips_14.htm

6. Information on "creating an effective PowerPoint presentation": http://people.csp.edu/saylor/effective_powerpoint.htm

TOPIC	**Teams** (teamwork, teambuilding, communicating in teams)

DEFINITION

Webster defines the noun *team* as "a group of people working or playing together" and the verb *team* as "to join in cooperative activity."

Teamwork is the cooperative/collaborative effort by members of a group to achieve a common goal.

KEY POINTS

1. Being a team player and having experience working in teams are highly valued skills by employers today.

2. The use of teams in organizations continues to increase as teamwork replaces the traditional way of doing business.
   a. Organizations continue to move toward team-based decision-making rather than individual-based decisions because teams consistently <u>outperform</u> individuals.
   b. The use of teams enables an organization to better utilize their resources and provides greater flexibility.
   c. The collective experiences and judgment of a team combined with the wide variety of skills far exceeds the talents of one individual.

3. Essentials of the team process are teambuilding, teamwork, leadership, and communication to create a collaborative effort to achieve a common goal.

4. Four stages of team development exist: forming, storming, norming, and performing. Understanding this evolutionary process of team development will help you to be a better team member.

   Stage 1 – Forming
   Initial formation of team:
   a. characterized by uncertainty with polite and tentative communication
   b. conflict is avoided
   c. goals are unclear and member roles not yet assigned
   d. must allow conflict to develop to lead to Stage 2.

Stage 2 – Storming
Team defines itself:
   a. characterized by disagreement and competition among team members to clarify roles and goals
   b. trust begins when conflicts are resolved which leads to Stage 3

Stage 3 – Norming
Teamwork and commitment to the group develops:
   a. characterized by mutual trust and matching of skills with tasks
   b. constructive feedback is given within the team
   c. communication and cohesion develop which leads to Stage 4

Stage 4 - Performing
Full-fledged team develops:
   a. characterized by cooperation, with effective communication among members and a clear understanding of the team's goals
   b. team is functioning as a sum of its parts and not as individuals
   c. leadership functions shift and are distributed among members as appropriate

5. Conflict is a natural and necessary part of the team process.
   a. "Good" conflict is referred to as *cognitive* conflict.
   b. Cognitive conflict is constructive by focusing on issues (not people or personalities).
   c. Conflict needs to occur to avoid groupthink.
   d. "Bad" conflict is referred to as *affective* conflict.
   e. Affective conflict is destructive because it focuses on people and personalities.

6. The best teams include the following characteristics:
   a. 5-7 diverse members
   b. Commitment to common purpose, goals, and procedures (all team members know what needs to be done, when, by whom, how, why.)
   c. Mutual respect, trust, and support
   d. Open communication; listen and share ideas
   e. Shared leadership/shared responsibility
   f. Efficient, productive meetings (collaboration)
   g. Conflict resolution (respect differences in others)
   h. Utilization of member resources and talents

7. Be sure you play a positive role in your team:
    a. Do not withdraw during meetings; participate in the team process.
    b. Ask questions and get clarification.
    c. Do not compete with other team members; be willing to collaborate and recognize the talents of others.
    d. Do not dominate discussion or ridicule ideas of others
    e. Contribute and complete your tasks as assigned.
    f. Agree to disagree; consensus is crucial in a team; you won't always get your way.

8. Research shows the top reasons the use of teams and the team process continues to increase in organizations are due to the following benefits:
    a. Better utilizes talents, time, and energy of employees
    b. Improves decision making and increases ownership of decisions
    c. Increases work capacity--more cost effective
    d. Increases employee morale

9. The major advantages of teams may be best explained by looking at the teamwork of geese as discussed in "Teambuilding Lessons We Can Learn from Geese" on the following page.

Teambuilding Lessons We Can Learn From Geese

Fact #1 – As each bird flaps its wings, it creates uplift for the bird following. By flying in a "V" formation, the whole flock adds 71 percent greater flying range than if one bird flew alone.

Lesson Learned – People who share a common direction and sense of community can get where they are going quicker and easier because they are traveling on the strength of one another.

Fact #2 – Whenever a goose falls out of formation, it suddenly feels the drag and resistance of trying to fly alone and quickly gets back into formation to take advantage of the lifting power of the bird immediately in front.

Lesson Learned – If we have as much sense as geese, we will stay in formation with those who are ahead of where we want to go and be willing to accept their help as well as give ours to others.

Fact #3 – When the lead goose gets tired, it rotates back into the formation and another goose flies at the point position.

Lesson Learned – It pays to take turns doing the hard tasks and sharing leadership.

Fact #4 – The geese in formation honk from behind to encourage those up front to keep up their speed.

Lesson Learned – We need to make sure our honking from behind is Encouraging--not something else.

Fact #5 – When a goose gets sick or wounded or shot down, two geese drop out of formation and follow it down to help and protect it. They stay with it until it is able to fly again--or dies. Then they launch out on their own, with another formation, or they catch up with their flock.

Lesson Learned – If we have as much sense as geese do, we too, will stand by each other in difficult times as well as when we are strong.

-Author Unknown.
(refer to http://teambuildinginc.com/article_geese.htm to print this article)

1. Learn more about the stages of team development by visiting the Virtual Team Assistant web site, Lesson 2: Stages of Team Development.

   a. Include printouts from this web site in your team's oral communications resource file. www.vta.spcomm.uiuc.edu/TBG/tbgt2-ov.html

2. Read more about teambuilding and related teambuilding issues. Check out the articles, resources, and links on a variety of teamwork related topics designed to help you develop an understanding of the team process.

3. Include printouts from these web sites in your team's oral communications resource file: www.vta.spcomm.uiuc.edu/, http://teambuildinginc.com/, and http://leadership.monster.com/

4. Form a team of three; prepare an outline for an oral presentation to inform (following the golden rule of oral presentations) on why interpersonal, leadership, and communication skills are considered "core management skills." Your main points will be:
   a. interpersonal skills
   b. leadership skills
   c. communication skills

5. Understanding your own personality traits and leadership style will help you to understand your own behavior, especially in a team environment and how you fit with other personality types in your team. Complete one of the following on-line tests:

   a. Complete the Jung-Meyers-Briggs typology test online at www.humanmetrics.com (click on "Jung typology test"). Print out your test results and the explanations about your personality type provided. Read about the other types so you have a better understanding of how differences in personality types affect our behavior and team dynamics.

6. Complete Monster.com's online quiz "Are You a Team Player" to determine how well you are cut out for teamwork: http://content.monster.com/tools/quizzes/teamplayer/

   a. Print out your test results, including the "analysis" of each question.

TOPIC **Intercultural communication**

DEFINITION Communicating with other peoples and other cultures both orally and in writing will be one of your tasks in the global office.

BACKGROUND Communicating with people from other cultures requires that you know a bit about contexting. People from *high-context* countries, like the Japanese and other Asians, seem vague when communicating. People in high-context countries use personal relationships as a way of doing business. People from high-context countries depend more on *how* you say or write something than on *what* you actually said or wrote. Speak or write to people in high-context countries using the *indirect* approach.

People from *low-context* countries, such as Germany, Holland, and many of the European countries, get right to the point in their oral and written communications. These people may seem rude, but they are not. Being brief and concise is the way they have learned to communicate over the years. Speak or write to people in low-context countries using the *direct* approach.

KEY POINTS

1. Determine whether the person you are writing or speaking to comes from a high- or low-context country.
    a. You can find this information by using the Internet or by going to your library.

2. Use expressions that are easily understood by people from other countries and other cultures.
    a. Avoid *idioms, clichés, slang, jargon, redundancies,* and *euphemisms;* avoid using contractions (an international person may not understand that the word *"won't,"* for instance, is a shortened form of *will not).*

3. Use short, simple sentences and short paragraphs.

4. Avoid discussing controversial items, such as war, poverty, politics, and the like.

5. Use a traditional format for letters; the block style letter is easily interpreted by people from other cultures.
    a. If you are interested in how people from a certain culture or country format their letters, you can contact your local United States Post Office for information about international formats.

6. Use graphics or pictures whenever possible to help get your point across.

7. Strive for clarity in both oral and written presentations.

8. Use correct grammar and punctuation.

9. Learn some simple foreign phrases and include one or two of them in your oral or written presentation.

10. Speak slowly and clearly.

11. Listen without interrupting when you are speaking to someone from another culture or another country.

12. Smile; be pleasant when speaking with international people.

13. Always remember, the meanings of nonverbal communication are culturally determined.
    a. Common forms of nonverbal communication such as eye contact, smiling, and a wave of your hand mean distinctly different things in different cultures.

ACTIVITIES

1. Consult the Internet and the library to get a list of idioms, clichés, slang, redundancies, and jargon.

    a. Prepare a short memo report summarizing and giving examples of what you have found (refer to Unit III, pages 93-94 for memo report format guidelines).

2. Meet with your teammates to complete your *team oral communication resource file* (part of the Capstone Project for this unit).

    a. Visit web sites that provide information on intercultural communications and printout information from these web sites to include in your team's resource file.

3. Learn more about cultural issues in business communication, cross-cultural communication, and examine cultural differences and similarities with an online tutorial at: www.bena.com/ewinters/culiss.html.

4. Checkout issues related to cultural differences at www.worldbiz.com.

5. Prepare an outline for a short oral presentation to report on a topic you or your instructor chooses for an audience from a high-context country.

   a. Give your oral presentation to the rest of your team members.

   b. Re-do the outline for an audience from a low-context country.

   c. Discuss what changes were made to adapt your presentations to the different audiences in your team or as a class.

   d. Turn in a copy of each outline as part of your Capstone Project for this unit.

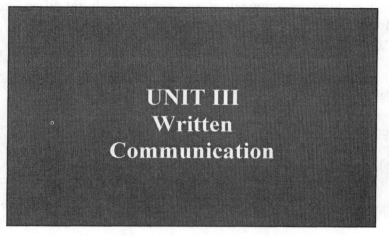

UNIT III
Written Communication

CAPSTONE PROJECT FOR WRITTEN COMMUNICATION UNIT III

The Capstone Project for Unit III is designed to apply the main topics in this unit into one integrated assignment. The integration of the unit topics via the completed assignments will result in a resource file that contains examples of common business documents. You will work in teams (your instructor will decide the number in each team) or as individuals to complete the following collaborative project. Prepare a copy of the final project for each team member to have as a resource tool for later use in your career. The project will consist of any or all of the following; however, your instructor will tell you which of the following items to include in the project:

1. Company letterhead with logo
2. Company letterhead for memo
3. Product brochure
4. Product advertisement (one- page print advertisement)
5. Persuasive sales letter
6. Progress report
7. Press release
8. Outline of oral presentation to inform or persuade
9. Peer evaluations
10. Two-sided business card
11. Writing of instructions
12. Code of ethics
13. Any other project required by your instructor

Instructions for Capstone Project:

1. Form teams and <u>elect</u> someone in your team to act as facilitator. The other members of the team are project members. The facilitator will keep the team on task.

2. Design a <u>company letterhead</u> for use in a fictitious company you have organized within your group. Use the Internet or other resources to come up with a design of your own making. Include a graphic for your company logo.

3. Design a <u>product</u> that your company will produce. Prepare a <u>memo</u> that includes a description of the product after your team has come to a final decision. Input is expected from all team members. Include information to answer the questions in the memo to your instructor:
    a. Who will use the product (the audience)?
    b. How does the product work?
    c. From what materials is the product made?
    d. What are the product's superior features in design and construction?
    e. What is the price? Is the price competitive?
    f. What kind of servicing will the product require?
    g. Are similar products available? If so, how does the product stack up against the competition?

4. Prepare a <u>brochure</u> that promotes your product to consumers.

5. Prepare a one-page <u>print advertisement</u> of the product that will be featured in business periodicals and in *USA Today*. Use both text and graphics. Use the A-I-D-A approach (see page 111).

6. Prepare a <u>persuasive sales letter</u> to introduce your new product or service. The letter will be duplicated and sent to over one million people in the United States and Canada. Use the A-I-D-A approach.

7. During the time you are working on this project, you will be asked to prepare a <u>progress report</u> on the status of your project at your instructor's discretion.

8. Prepare a <u>press release</u> to announce the availability of your new product or service.

9. Prepare an <u>outline</u> for an oral presentation to inform or persuade to your class about your product.

10. Prepare a <u>two-sided business card.</u> One side of the business card will have your name, address, and other information. The other side of the business

card will include a mini-resume of your accomplishments (see the *Appendix,* page 219 also).

11. Give a <u>team presentation</u> of your product utilizing appropriate visual aids. Your instructor will assign the time frame.

12. Complete <u>peer evaluations</u> of the other members of your team when the entire project is completed. A peer evaluation form is included in the *Appendix,* page 203.

13. <u>Submit all requirements</u> your instructor requests for this Capstone Project. Be sure your materials are presented to your instructor in an attractive and professional format.

Note for additional assignments: A memo format quiz and letter format quiz are included in the *Appendix,* pages 210 and 211.

TOPIC   **Using the writing process—preparing to write**

DEFINITION   Do not start writing until you have planned what you are to do. The writing process consists of (1) planning; (2) composing, drafting and revising; (3) formatting; and (4) editing, proofing, and evaluating.

BACKGROUND   The fact is that people write in many different ways. You probably have your own plan for writing, and that is good. No matter what source you check out to see how to write, you will probably find that each source is basically the same.

According to many studies over the past several years, employers are looking for employees who can write. In fact, one of the most valued skills by employers, according to recruiters, is for employees who can deliver a positive impression of the company through business writing. Memos, letters, and reports will represent the company to the outside world. If you want to climb the corporate ladder, you must learn how to write effectively.

KEY POINTS

1. **Planning**. Determine to whom the message is to be sent. What information will you need to give the reader?

2. **Composing, drafting, and revising**. After you have written down your plan, start composing what you are going to say. You will probably use one of the plans listed in this text as your guide. You probably will not get the letter ready for mailing until you have revised it several times.

3. **Formatting**. Keyboard the letter after you are entirely satisfied with what you have said and that you are certain the reader will know exactly what you mean.

4. **Editing and proofing**. Spend at least the same amount of time editing and proofing as you did on writing the letter—perhaps even more time editing and proofing. Find all errors. Make all corrections. Get someone else to proofread your work.

STEPS

1. Analyze your audience. To whom are you writing? You will structure your communication differently when writing to young people as opposed to writing to older people. What do you know about the receiver? What about the cultural background of the receiver?

2. Determine the purpose for writing.
   a. What do you want to accomplish and what can you do to achieve that purpose?
   b. Is your purpose realistic?
   c. Is your purpose timely?

3. Organize your thoughts.
   a. Prepare an outline of what you want to accomplish in the communication. Even before you prepare an outline, you may wish just to jot down some random ideas as these ideas appear to you.
   b. After you have written down a variety of random thoughts, organize those thoughts into a coherent plan. Some possible methods of organization are the following:

      1) Organize data by time. Arrange information chronologically.
      2) Organize data by classification: location, geography, division, section, product, service, or part.
      3) Organize data from most important to least important.
      4) Organize data from least important to most important.
      5) Organize data by categories, such as price, warranty, speed, print quality, and so forth.
      6) Organize data according to prescribed categories, such as personnel, budget, and so forth.

4. Write a first draft.
   a. Put your ideas into paragraph form. Be prepared to write several drafts before you come up with a final draft.
   b. Write concise paragraphs. Business writing should be brief. Comprehension rates decrease the longer the sentence (refer to the "rule of eights" for writing, page 88).

5. Proofread and edit.
   a. Expect to spend about half of your time (or sometimes even more) on proofreading, editing, rewriting, and revising before your document becomes the final draft.

6. A good rule for checking your work is to use the list below. Note that every word starts with the letter "C". These "C's of business communication" become easy to remember and should be applied in all of your business writing. A check list for the "C's of Business Communication" appears in the *Appendix*, page 215 also.

   a. **Character/Consideration/Confidence.** Use the YOU attitude in your writing. Make the reader feel as though you are talking directly to him or her. Use the reader's name in the communication whenever possible: (Thank you, Ms. Cummings, for the fine work you did on the project.) Respond to any communication you receive promptly—usually within three days, if possible. Use a positive tone rather than a negative one. Use "please" and "thank you" frequently. Use gender-fair and unbiased language. Treat everyone with equal respect.

   b. **Conciseness/Concreteness.** Be specific, not vague. Avoid wordiness. Give essential information in as few words as possible. Avoid redundancies, idioms, clichés, euphemisms, slang, and jargon. Use short words; use short sentences and short paragraphs.

   c. **Correctness/Completeness.** Use proper grammar and standard mechanics. Check spelling and punctuation. Proofread and edit. Then proofread and edit again. Reading the letter aloud can point out errors you never knew you had.

   d. **Conversational Tone.** Use a friendly, helpful approach in business communications. Write as though you were speaking directly to someone. Picture the person or the person's business position in your mind as you write.

   e. **Clarity.** Use vivid, understandable language. Your writing must not only be CLEAR—but be UNMISTAKABLE. Two writing rules that will help you out are the following:

7. **Rule of Primacy.** The rule of primacy is known as the rule of firsts. That which comes first gets the most emphasis. Place your most important idea to the *left* of the verb in the sentence. Example:

   a. *Poor sentence:* **There will be a meeting today.** The verb is "will be"; according to the rule of primacy, the word to the left of the verb is considered as the most important word in the sentence—and "there" certainly is not the most important word in the sentence. Unimportant words are called "expletives." Avoid expletives. Avoid the expletive "it" when "it" appears to the left of the verb.

   b. *Better sentence:* **The meeting will be held today.** The word to the left of the verb is "meeting," which is probably the most important word in the sentence.

8. **Rule of Recency.** The rule of recency says that the information that appears near the end of the sentence is the *second most important* place of emphasis in a business communication. Example:

   a. **The meeting will be held today.** The rule of primacy says the most important word is the word "meeting"; but the rule of recency says the next most important word is "today," because "today" appears near the end of the sentence (actually, the word appears at the end of the sentence, which is even better).

   b. **The board of directors hired a new CEO.** Rule of primacy: *important* - board of directors; *verb* - hired; rule of recency - *new CEO.* The "board of directors" gets the *most* emphasis in the sentence; the "new CEO" gets the *second-most* emphasis in the sentence. If you think the CEO is the most important item in the sentence, then rewrite the sentence to conform to the rule of primacy.

   c. **A new CEO was hired by the board of directors.** Now, you have given the "new CEO" the most prominence in the sentence and "board of directors" the second-most important spot in the sentence.

9. Define "demonstrative" pronouns (or words that *point out*). Four demonstrative pronouns are used in business writing regularly: *this, that, these,* and *those*. For added clarity in your writing, **define** the demonstrative pronoun; in other words, **place a noun after a demonstrative pronoun** for even more clarity:

   a. Give me those (not clear).
   b. Give me those *plans*. (clear)

   c. Those belong to Amy. (not clear)
   d. Those *books* belong to Amy. (clear)

   e. This is beautiful. (not clear)
   f. This *day* is beautiful. (clear)

   g. These will never work. (not clear)
   h. These *processes* will never work. (clear)

10. Use proper sentence patterns for effective and clear communication.

    a. *Simple sentences.* Simple sentences contain one independent clause; that is, a subject and verb that can stand alone as a correct sentence and create a single idea. Simple sentences are used for **creating emphasis** and **getting the reader's attention**: (1) *The winter storm was scary.* (2) *Georgia was promoted to manager.* (3) *We must stop this silliness.*

    b. *Compound sentences.* A compound sentence contains two or more independent clauses (sentences) joined by a comma and a conjunction (and, but, for, nor, or so, yet) or by a semicolon alone. Use a compound sentence to create a balanced relationship between the clauses that are joined. Your writing will then emphasize the idea that both clauses are somewhat equal in importance: (1) *We moved to Florida in 1999,* **but** *we stayed only five years.* (2) *Mary is an excellent manager; John is not an excellent manager.* (3) *The reports were late,* **and** *the entire team was fired.*

11. *Complex sentences.* A complex sentence contains at least two clauses: one independent and one or more subordinate clauses. A complex sentence is used to relate ideas to each other. Use a complex sentence in business writing to subordinate *bad news*

to the reader. **The *bad news* is placed in the subordinate clause, and the good news follows in the independent clause:**

   (a) *Although James failed the final examination, he passed the course.*
   (b) *If you find that you cannot pay the entire amount at this time, please pay only the interest portion of the bill.*
   (c) *He knew that he was ill, but the doctor has great hopes for his full recovery.*

12. *Compound-complex sentences.* A compound-complex sentence contains three or more clauses—at least two independent clauses and one subordinate clause. Use a compound-complex sentence to establish a series of complicated relationships among a series of ideas. Many times this type of sentence is used to "de-emphasize" bad news to the reader:

   (a) *When we lived in Alaska, we survived the extremely cold weather; but we never felt that we were in danger from the cold.*
   (b) *Because I do not believe him, I feel for the safety of his children; the authorities have been notified to keep a close watch on the entire family.*
   (c) *If you ever get to Michigan, be sure to stop to see me; and we will spend a few days fishing in Lake Michigan.*

ACTIVITIES

1. Search the Internet to find examples of redundancies, idioms, clichés, euphemisms, slang, and jargon. Find at least three examples of each. Compose sentences for each of the words. Submit the results of your research to your instructor in memo format.

2. Write ten sentences that illustrate the correct use of demonstrative pronouns. Submit the sentences to your instructor in memo format.

3. Find a one-page article from a news magazine (*Time, Newsweek, U.S. News and World Report*, or others). Make a copy of the article. Then search the article for violations of the rule of primacy and the rule of recency. Discuss your findings in groups of two or three.

4. Bring a business letter you may have received recently to class. Analyze the business letter for the many items talked about in

this section. Discuss the letter with two or three others. Prepare a team memo for your instructor. Attach the letter you analyzed.

5. Search the Internet or the library to find a list of common misspelled business words. Make a list of the words, correctly spelled. Use the list whenever you have some writing to do.

6. Study the punctuation, capitalization, and number writing rules that appear in Unit IV of the text. Be prepared for short quizzes on punctuation, capitalization, and number writing rules.

7. You may want to practice some exercises on eliminating expletives and on defining demonstrative pronouns. Turn to pages 216-218 in the *Appendix* for this additional practice.

8. What does the term *noun phrase* mean? Some additional terms that you need to know are the following: *independent clause, dependent clause, subordinate clause*, Use the Internet to find a definition and some examples of all these terms. Prepare a short memo to your instructor describing your findings.

9. Write five of each of the following sentences: *simple sentences, compound sentences, complex sentences,* and *compound-complex sentences.* Make the sentences business related. Attach the sentences to a short memo and submit the material to your instructor.

RESOURCES

www.junketstudies.com/index.htmldies.com: discusses 11 rules of writing; includes tutorials.

http://webster.commnet.edu/grammar/: provides a thorough guide to grammar and writing.

www.bartlelby.com: lists many of the rules of writing.

www.mantex.co.uk: provides an opportunity to subscribe to a free newsletter on the rules for writing well.

TOPIC   **Grammar and punctuation guidelines**

DEFINITION   The word "grammar" comes from a Greek word, *grammatikos,* which means "knowing one's language." Grammar is more than just a list of rules; grammar helps in understanding both the written word and oral speech.

BACKGROUND   Grammar often refers to the correct or standard way to use the language. Business communication embodies a list of what is appropriate and what is not appropriate in the business world. Grammar makes clear the exact meaning of what is being said. Knowing the fundamentals of grammar is extremely helpful in business communication.

KEY POINTS

1. In order to improve your writing skills, you must have a solid foundation of grammar and punctuation rules.
   a. Effective business writing is concise writing that follows rules.
   b. Always use the "KISS" principle (Keep It Short and Simple) for the best business writing.

2. Remember the **"rule of eights"** for writing:
   a. The longer a sentence, the lower the rate of comprehension, according to the American Press Institute.
   b. Short, concise sentences consisting of **eight** words have the highest comprehension rate (100 percent); a sentence of 28 words in length has a comprehension rate of only 50 percent.
   c. The best length for a paragraph is less than **eight** lines.
   d. An effective paragraph discusses only one topic.
   e. For most writing, a paragraph is written in the direct pattern, with the main idea stated in the first sentence.

ACTIVITIES and RESOURCES

1. Improve your knowledge of the rules of grammar and punctuation as well as your writing skills by reviewing these online grammar and punctuation resources and online quizzes:

   a. The on-line sites provide answers to your grammar and punctuation questions; determine word, sentence, and paragraph levels as well as essay and research paper level: http://ccc.commnet.edu/grammar/

b. Visit the Grammar Lady web site maintained by a retired English professor; provides answers to your grammar and punctuation questions online or by phone with a toll-free number: www.grammarlady.com

c. The "Pop-up Grammar" web site provides online grammar quizzes with pop-up answers and explanations: www.brownlee.org/durk/grammar/

d. The "Grammar Help" web site, interactive exercises, and tons of resources: www.ruthvilmi.net/hut/help/grammar_help/

e. Check out this web site that provides hundreds of business writing tips: http://writing-reading.com/tips-index.htm

f. This web site offers a basic explanation of effective for beginners, including format information and proper tone: www.webfoot.com/advice/.top.html#intro.

g. WordDog is an online editor that reviews your document and suggests changes for improvement; also provides links to online dictionaries, encyclopedias, and quotations: www.worddog.com/

h. Access an online dictionary or Roget's Thesaurus plus links to hundreds of other online dictionaries, including non-English dictionaries: www.dictionary.com

i. Build your vocabulary at "A Word a Day" web site; once you subscribe you'll receive each day's word via email (you'll receive a new vocabulary word email each weekday): http://wordsmith.org/awad/index.html

TOPIC **Preparing an outline**

DEFINITION An outline is a visual presentation of an assignment you are about to complete. Outlining helps you to organize your thoughts and gives you a chance to look at the overall picture before you begin the actual task. Writing from an outline makes your writing go more smoothly and saves time.

STEPS

1. Prepare a report; use the report title as the main title, center all caps at the top. Keep the heading specific.

2. Use upper-case roman numerals for the main headings of your outline (I, II, III, etc.)

3. Second-level headings may be numeric (1, 2, 3, etc.) or upper case alphabetic (A, B, C, etc.) depending on your style and word processing program.

4. Third-level subheadings may be lower case alphabetic (a, b, c, etc.), or numeric (depending on what type of second-level headings were used). You want to alternate between alphabetic and numeric throughout the different levels of your outline.

5. Have at least two items under each heading or subheading. You may not have to use a second or third subheading, but you should know how to organize a very detailed outline.

6. Use parallel phrasing in the headings. Use all noun phrases or all participial phrases, all statements, or all questions.

7. Be consistent within each level of heading. If the first words are a noun phrase, then all of the first words should be noun phrases.

ACTIVITIES

1. Search the Internet and the library for a variety of ways to prepare an outline. Present the results in memo format to your instructor and discuss your preference for preparing an outline.

2. Find out the meaning of "brainstorming." How does brainstorming help you in your writing? Pick a topic with a partner and see how many ideas each of you can come up with in 30 seconds or in one minute.

3. Using the Internet or the library, find a company yearly report. Study the report carefully; then prepare an outline of the report. Hand in the outline to your instructor.

4. Select an article two or more pages in length from a current magazine. Read the article carefully. Then prepare an outline of the article you have read. Hand in both the article and the outline to your instructor.

5. Check the Internet and the library to see techniques other than brainstorming for developing ideas for writing. Make a list of these techniques, each with a short description; and submit the list to your instructor in a memo.

6. In one of the lecture classes you attend, prepare an outline of the day's presentation *after* you have listened to the lecture.

7. In the sample outline that follows, rewrite the outline so that each of the items is parallel within its category.

8. Choose an area of business you may be interested in becoming employed. Search the Internet and the library for "jargon" in your area. Write a short memo to your instructor that includes ten items of jargon along with the actual meaning of the word or of the term.

RESOURCES

http://www.mnstate.edu/wasson/ed603/ed603lesson5.htm: discusses how to prepare and outline and write the literature review.

http://www.hazlet.org/resources/index.shtml: provides multiple writing-related resources, including grammar, researching and writing a paper, using an outline as a basis for organizing a paper; steps for preparing an outline, and "ask an expert."

http://webster.commnet.edu/mla/outlines.shtml: provides material on preparing outlines.

PLAN FOR NEW OFFICE CONFERENCE CALLS

Reginald Dennis

I.   INTRODUCTION

    A. Background of Problem
    B. Purpose of Redefining Costs
    C. Preliminary Procedures

II.   OBJECTIVES OF NEW
    PROCEDURES

    A.   No setup fees
    B.   No contracts or monthly fees
    C.   Call anytime
        1. From anywhere
        2. To anywhere

III. BENEFITS

    A.   Up to 150 participants at any one time
    B.   International calls at 15 cents per minute
    C.   Simplicity in set up and administration
    D.   Operator help available 24/7
    E.   Cost savings will show up almost immediately

IV.   AVAILABILITY

    A.   Begins May 1, 200x
        1. Call extension 343
            a.   Give your name to receptionist
            b.   Ask for Form 45-B
        2. Alert your private secretary

TOPIC	**Preparing a memo**

DEFINITION　　A memorandum (memo) is an *internal* communication, whereas a business letter is an *external* communication. A memo is used to disseminate day-to-day information within the company. (See example on page 94.)

BACKGROUND　　Memos are usually written on a type of abbreviated company stationery. Usually, a memo is preprinted with standard headings that can be arranged in a variety of ways and include: TO: FROM: DATE: and SUBJECT. Many software packages include a memo template for your use.

KEY POINTS

1. Fill in the information for the headings (headings may be preprinted). Be sure to align the information as shown in the example memo on page 94.

2. Salutations and complimentary closes are not used in memos. "Sign" your memo by initialing at your typed name on the "FROM" line in your memo heading.

3. Use a triple space between the SUBJECT line and your first paragraph.

4. Use block format. Single-space within each paragraph in the memo, but double space between the paragraphs.

5. Use the same organizational format that you use in letters; for instance, write the memo in *direct* style if the memo contains good news; write the memo in *indirect* style if the memo contains unfavorable news.

ACTIVITIES

1. Write a memo to all staff members congratulating each of them on the fine showing the company made in contributions to the United Way. Over $17,000 was collected from the 85 employees.

2. Write a memo to all staff members telling them that the day after Thanksgiving will be a workday. No one is to get the Friday off as a day of vacation.

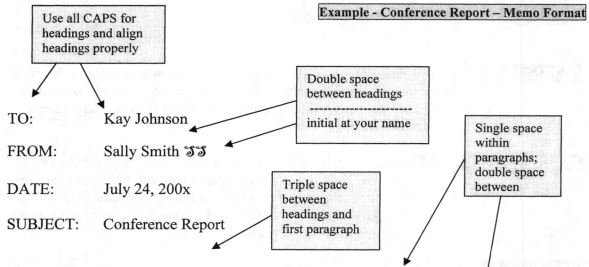

TO: Kay Johnson

FROM: Sally Smith 𝒮𝒮

DATE: July 24, 200x

SUBJECT: Conference Report

I recently attended the Academy of Business Administration Conference in San Antonio, Texas, to learn more about cultural diversity issues in the workplace. My overall impression of the conference was very positive. The following two topics were the focus of the session I attended on cultural diversity:

- Legal ramifications and liabilities to the business should be of paramount concern to upper management. Personnel in management positions should be trained in all areas related to these issues via seminars provided by legal professionals.

- Employee sensitivity to cultural issues in the workplace can provided for through cultural awareness training seminars. Each business should conduct assessments of cultural issues in the workplace to determine needs and issues to target in providing training.

I would be happy to share more information with you regarding the conference and what I feel would help our company to be successful in dealing with cultural diversity issues. Please contact me at your earliest convenience to schedule a meeting.

Letter style formats

Several different **letter styles** are used in business today. The most popular of these styles is the *full-block letter style*, where every line of the letter begins at the left margin. Another favorite letter style is the *modified-block* letter style, where every line begins at the left margin *except* the date line, the complimentary close, and the signature line, which begin at or near the center of the paper.

Still another often-used letter style is the letter created by the Administrative Management Society (AMS). The AMS style letter does not have a salutation or a complimentary closing and is good for writing letters when the reader's name is not available.

Punctuation styles fall into two categories. *Open punctuation,* which means no colon appears after the salutation and no comma appears after the complimentary closing. *Mixed punctuation* means that a colon appears after the salutation and a comma appears after the complimentary closing. Mixed punctuation continues to be one of the most popular styles of punctuation used in business offices.

KEY POINTS   1. Full-block letters may use either mixed punctuation or open punctuation. Every line in a full-block style letter begins at the left margin (see example, page 97).

2. Modified-block style letters may use either mixed punctuation or open punctuation. Modified-block letters may either have indented paragraphs or blocked paragraphs (see example, page 98).

3. The AMS-style letter uses open punctuation. All lines begin at the left margin (see example, page 99).

ACTIVITIES and RESOURCES

1. Use the Internet or the library to find an article about the importance of written business communication. Find information about the other letter formats like full-block style letter, the modified-block style letter, and the AMS-style letter. Discuss your findings with the class.

2. Collect various letter styles and bring to class for discussion.

3. Research other letter styles. Write a memo to your instructor with your findings. Present findings orally to the class.

4. Check out some of the following web sites. Write a memo to your instructor with your findings.

   www.research.umbc.edu: discusses three formats commonly used for writing business letters.

   http://englishplus.com/grammar/letrcont.htm: shows what a one-page business letter should look like.

   http://jobsearchtech.about.com/: shows various styles of letters that can be downloaded and much more.

5. The quality of the paper you use for your letterheads in the office is important. Use the Internet and find out all you can about letterheads and the quality of paper used for them. Prepare a short memo to your instructor with your findings. Cite the web sites as the last item in your memo.

6. Find information on the Internet about the addressing of envelopes for business letters. Should the envelopes be of the same high quality as the letter paper? Prepare a short report for your instructor. Be prepared to present your findings orally to the class.

✦Company Letterhead✦

November 12, 200x

Ms. Lorraine Beatty
Beatty Hair Styling Salon
987 West Harrison Street
Glendale, CA 98798

Dear Ms. Beatty

This letter is an example of the full-block style with open punctuation. Please note that *all* lines in this letter begin at the left-hand margin. This style is a good one to use because you do not have to remember to indent paragraphs or other lines in the letter.

The material in each paragraph is single spaced, but you need to be sure to leave an extra space between paragraphs. This extra space is called *double spacing*. Note also that an extra blank line exists *before* and *after* the salutation (Dear Ms. Beatty). The only place you may vary the spacing of the letter is between the date and the inside address. If you have a short letter, leave space between the date and inside address that will cause the letter to look centered on the page. If you have a long letter, leave less space between the date and the inside address. Note that the person you are sending the letter to is part of what is known as the *inside address*.

The letter also illustrates *open* punctuation. Open punctuation means no colon appears after the salutation and no comma appears after the complimentary closing. An *enclosure notation* is placed below the signature line when something is included with the letter.

I hope you appreciate the information in this letter and the attached rules of writing. Good luck in writing all of your letters. Be sure to proofread and edit carefully.

Sincerely yours

Bob Hatchett

Bob Hatchett

Enclosure

✦Company Letterhead✦

November 11, 200x

Mr. Johnstone Bigelow
987 North Sawyer Boulevard
Canton, OH 44238

> If necessary, you can reduce the number of spaces after the date line for longer letters so they fit on one page

Dear Mr. Bigelow:

This letter is an example of the modified-block style. Modified-block style means that the date line and the closing lines begin at the center point of the page. In the modified-block style letter, *you may or you may not* indent the paragraphs. The choice is yours.

This letter also illustrates the use of *mixed* punctuation. Mixed punctuation means that a colon is placed after the salutation (Dear Mr. Bigelow:) and that a comma is placed after the complimentary close (Sincerely,). In any style letter you write, you have a choice of using mixed or open punctuation. I chose to use mixed punctuation in this letter.

Some other facts about letters that may be helpful to you are the following: (Note, too, that you may use "bullets" to highlight certain information. Bullets may be indented to call attention to them.)

- The name and address of the person to whom you are writing is the *inside address.*

- The greeting at the top of the letter (Dear Mr. Bigelow) is the *salutation.*

- The body of the letter is made up of *paragraphs.* One blank line is included between the paragraphs.

- The *complimentary close* (Sincerely) appears at the bottom of the letter above the writer's signature.

- The *signature line* is typed four returns down from the complimentary close. Write your name above the printed name.

This information should be helpful to you as you continue to write business letters.

Sincerely,

Ima Wright

Ima Wright

✦Company Letterhead✦

December 15, 200x

The Michigan Letter Writing Corporation
12345 Lansing Street
Grand Rapids, MI   49879

SAMPLE OF AMS-STYLE LETTER

This letter is an example of the AMS-style. AMS stands for Administrative Management Society. This style is a simplified way of sending letters and is especially good when you have a company name and address but do not know the reader's name.

Note that no salutation appears in the letter. The *subject* of the letter (SAMPLE OF AMS-STYLE LETTER) appears in ALL CAPITAL letters three spaces below the inside address. Then the first paragraph of the letter begins three spaces below the subject line.

Full-block style is used in the AMS letter. Since no salutation or complimentary close exists, you don't have to worry about open or mixed punctuation.

At the bottom of the letter, you will note that no complimentary closing exists. However, the typed signature with the writer's title is typed in ALL CAPS five spaces down from the last line of the last paragraph (LOUISE H. WHEELMAN—OFFICE MANAGER).

I hope you enjoy this little bit of information about the AMS-Style letter. You may have occasion to use the letter in the future.

Louise H. Wheelman

LOUISE H. WHEELMAN—OFFICE MANAGER

TOPIC **Preparing a letter or memo in direct style**

DEFINITION Direct style is used for "good news" letters; such as, letters of congratulations, order letters, request letters, favorable responses, routine inquires, and simple claim letters. Good news letters are relatively short as letters go. Most letters written for business are short—perhaps 75 words or less. The direct style may be used for memos as well as for letters.

BACKGROUND Letters are typed on company stationery. Begin with the date. Use a full-block letter style; that is, every line begins at the *left margin*. The full-block letter style is one of the most popular letter styles used in business.

STEPS Three sections are included in a *direct style* letter:

1. **The objective.** The first section (usually one paragraph) should contain the good news for the reader: "Congratulations on your promotion." "Please send me the following items immediately." "Thank you for your kind words of sympathy."

2. **Facts, information, data, reasons.** The second section of the direct plan gives any information or factual material that will support the objective in Step 1. Use as many paragraphs as you need in order to give the reader all the information. "Your thirty years at our company reflect well on you." "Your speaking of Sam so highly was comforting to me."

3. **Courteous closing.** Close courteously. Perhaps add a forward-looking statement. "We look forward to working another thirty years with you." "Your kindness to Sam and to me will never be forgotten."

ACTIVITIES

1. Write a congratulatory letter to one of your friends who has achieved some special honor or award recently.

2. The full-block letter style is only one of many. Find other letter styles on the Internet or in the library. Prepare to discuss your findings with the class.

3. In a business letter, a colon is placed after the salutation (Dear Mr. Budka:) and a comma is placed after the complimentary closing (Sincerely,). This type of punctuation is called *mixed punctuation*. Find other styles of punctuation used in business correspondence. Report your findings to the class.

4. Using the Internet and the library, find the types of punctuation used in business correspondence from at least three countries other than the United States. Prepare a memo of your findings for your instructor.

5. Send a direct memo to one of your co-workers expressing appreciation for an assigned job well done.

6. You have decided to attend graduate school. After studying the graduate catalog, you have narrowed your list of possibilities to three universities; but you are leaning toward attending Mid-State University in Ohio. Write a direct letter asking for all of the specific information you will need to know before you make your final decision. Some questions you want answered are as follows:

   a. Approximately how much time is necessary to get the graduate degree? One year? Two years?
   b. Are graduate assistantships available? If so, how does one go about getting an assistantship?
   c. What are the grade-point-average requirements for getting a Master of Business Administration (MBA) degree?
   d. How many graduate credits can be transferred to the MBA program from another institution?

You may have additional questions for which you need answers. Write the letter to the following person:

        Dr. Naomi Parks, Chair
        Department of Finance
        Mid-State University
        Pataskala, OH 43987

Regina Clause

604 E. Wisconsin Boulevard   Gaylord, MI 49431

OOOOOOOOOOOOOOOOOOOOOOOOOOOOOOOOOOOOOOOOOOOOOO

September 1, 200x

Mr. Robert T. Glockendorf, Sales Manager
The Independent Trailblazer Company
30987 West Georgia Boulevard
Cleveland, OH 43987

Dear Mr. Glockendorf:

Please send by UPS the following items from your fall catalog:

Description	Quantity	Price	Total Price
RJY Guitar	1	$475.59	$475.59
Guitar picks	5	30.00	150.00
G String	4	15.00	60.00
D String	5	15.00	75.00
Total			$760.59

My check for $760.59 is attached to this letter, and I look forward to receiving the merchandise as soon as possible.

Very truly yours,

Regina Clause

Regina Clause

Enclosure

✦Company Letterhead✦

August 31, 200x

Ms. Gretchen Long, Director
Library Services
Central Michigan University
Mount Pleasant, MI 48859

Dear Ms. Long:

Would you please answer the following questions for me about how to list citations in a yearly report? Here are some of the questions I have:

a. How are Internet references cited in the footnotes of a report?
b. How are Internet references cited in the bibliography of a report?
c. Is it necessary to have a bibliography in a report if footnotes are used?
d. Are references from books, magazines, and other reports still cited in MLA format?
e. Do any businesses use the APA style of footnoting?

Your answers to these questions are desperately needed. You may write or call me at your convenience.

Sincerely,

Rachel Wardrop

Rachel Wardrop, Director
Reports and Services

TO: Irene Clare, Assistant Manager
               Marketing Department

FROM: Rochelle S. Grafton, Manager *RSG*
               Marketing Department

DATE: August 1, 200x

SUBJECT: YOUR MUCH-DESERVED PROMOTION

Congratulations, Irene, on your promotion to Assistant Manager of the Marketing Department.

Your work for us within the department has been consistently outstanding over the nine years you have been with us.

I look forward to working more closely with you and hope that you are with us for many more years.

✦**Company Letterhead**✦

August 1, 200x

Mr. Ronnie Potts
1234 North Arizona Avenue
Sacramento, CA 98798

Dear Mr. Potts:

Yes, we will grant your claim for $45.98 you paid for a brand new garden hose that turned out to be full of holes.

We are sorry for the troubles you had with the hose, especially when it emptied too much water on your prize-winning pansies. Therefore, we are sending you a $500 gift certificate to replace the $195 worth of pansies destroyed.

We value your business, Mr. Potts, and hope that you will continue to purchase our products.

As a token of our appreciation for your business with us in the past, here is an additional coupon worth $50 off on your next order of garden flowers.

Sincerely,

Ima Dahl

Ima Dahl, Manager

Enclosures

TOPIC	**Preparing a letter in indirect style**
DEFINITION	Indirect writing style is used for giving "unfavorable news"; such as, not getting a promotion, not getting a bonus, being fired by the company, and other letters that give bad or unfavorable news. The goal of the writer is to keep the reader's goodwill and to get the reader to accept the unfavorable news. (See example on page 108.)
EXPLANATION	Indirect letters or memos are typed on company stationery. Begin with the date. Use a full-block letter style; that is, every line begins at the *left margin*. The full-block letter style is one of the most popular letter styles.
KEY POINTS	Four sections are included in an *indirect style* letter:

1. **The buffer** (1st paragraph). A buffer is a neutral opening that does not give a hint that the bad news is coming. Topics in this section of the letter could be any of the following: best news, compliment, appreciation, agreement, facts, or understandings.

2. **Reasons, explanation, facts** (2nd paragraph). The writer leads up to the bad news by cautiously listing the causes or the reasons for the unfavorable news before actually stating the bad news. Other topics the writer could cover are reader or other benefits, company policy explanation, positive words, or evidence that the matter was considered fairly. Depending on the reasons and explanation, you may have one or more paragraphs in this section.

3. **Unfavorable news** (embedded in 2nd paragraph). Give a clear statement of the unfavorable news. Give an alternative, if applicable. Use embedded placement; do not place the bad news as the first or the last item in the sentence. You may also *imply* a refusal rather than *state* the refusal outright. Perhaps you could come to a compromise with the reader. You may place the unfavorable news as an embedded item in the 2nd paragraph. If you do, be sure to have another sentence or two after the bad news so that the bad news is truly embedded.

4. **Close** (final paragraph). Give a forward-looking statement. Give information about the alternative you may have suggested. Offer your good wishes. Try to re-sell the reader on another idea if applicable. Close on a pleasant note.

1. You have received a letter from a good customer of yours asking for a copy of your sales catalogs for the past five years. You have copies for yourself and your employees, but you do not have any extra copies to send to customers. Write a letter in the indirect style telling the customer you cannot fulfill the request. You may wish to suggest an alternative to the customer.

2. Write a memorandum to one of your employees telling that employee that he or she has not been at the company long enough to receive the yearly Christmas bonus.

3. Write an indirect memo to your employees telling them that the union has instituted a no-smoking policy inside the building effectively immediately. Suggest alternatives to your employees.

4. Respond to a letter from a person seeking a job with your company. Currently, you have no position available for a person in Marketing Research, nor do you anticipate that you will have an opening in the near future. No money is available for personnel. You know, however, that Seymour Company in your city is looking for someone in Marketing Research. You do appreciate the letter, and you are eager to help. Write the letter to the following person:

   Ms. Claudia Polkenstein
   30987 North Clare Avenue
   Mount Pleasant, MI   48858

5. The local branch of the Independent Party wants to use your company auditorium for a rally they plan to hold in about six months. You do not want to get involved in any political activities. Write a letter to the chair of the Independent Party in your city telling that person the reasons you cannot permit the party to hold a rally in your company auditorium.

✦Company Letterhead✦

April 12, 200x

Ms. Irene Carrarra
Apartment 234
9874 West Main Street
Clare, MI 48853

Dear Ms. Carrarra:

Your business with us over the past ten years has been very much appreciated. We always look forward to serving you in our store. Thank you for being such a loyal customer.

1st paragraph - the buffer

2nd paragraph - reasons and explanations given before bad news

Our merchandise was available for inspection before you purchased it. Because the merchandise you ordered was sold "as-is" and without a refund policy, we cannot grant your request for replacement. Please understand our position and our policy.

In order to keep your goodwill, here is a coupon worth $25 on your next purchase from our store.

Thanks again for being such a loyal and caring customer over the years. We hope to continue to do business with you in the future.

Sincerely,

Richard Thomas

Richard Thomas
Accounts Receivable

Enclosure

TO: Harlan Preachman

FROM: Jessica Dowd, Director _JD_
                Human Resources Department

DATE: October 1, 200x

SUBJECT: YOUR REQUEST FOR PROMOTION

Thank you, Harlan, for the ten years you have been working with our company. You have been a loyal employee and have done your best with us.

Several people were considered for the promotion to director of your area. Two of the three people considered along with you have been here at least five years longer than you have. They, too, have been very loyal and dedicated to the company. Therefore, your request for promotion will be considered again next year; and, at that time, we see a great possibility that you will then receive the promotion.

Thank you again for applying for the promotion. We look forward to receiving your request next year at this time. Your dedication, loyalty, and creativity with this company, Harlan, are very much appreciated.

✦Company Letterhead✦

May 1, 200x

Ms. Geraldine Pagemaker
987 North Calcutta Boulevard
Kent, OH 44240

Dear Ms. Pagemaker:

As a loyal customer of ours for the past twenty years, your business is very much appreciated. We have received your request for reimbursement of the latest order of plants you bought from us.

Because the asters were on a closeout sale and because we had marked the asters "as-is," we cannot refund your money because the asters died after only six weeks in the ground.

However, because we value your business, here is a coupon for $25 off on your next order of plants. Please be assured that we appreciate your loyalty, and we want to keep you as a customer for many years to come.

Sincerely,

Robert Moab

Robert Moab, President

Enclosure

TOPIC	**Preparing a persuasive sales letter**

DEFINITION	Persuasive communications are used to sell products and services and to persuade someone to do something.

EXPLANATION

1. Persuasive communications use a definite plan to get the point across. One plan is called the A-I-D-A plan. In this plan, four distinct sections are included:

    A → Attention
    I → Interest
    D → Desire
    A → Action

2. Several methods are used to attract ATTENTION in beginning the letter:
    a. Ask a question.
    b. Start the letter with a solution to a problem.
    c. Use a news announcement.
    d. Begin with a quote from a famous person.
    e. Use an analogy—compare something unknown with something known.
    f. Use an "If" opening or a "What if" opening.
    g. Use a pun or a play on words.
    h. Use the "You have been selected to. . ." approach.

3. After getting the reader's attention in a *short* paragraph, move on to the INTEREST section:

    a. Describe the product or service. Tell all you know about the product or service, such as size, color, shape, weight, etc.
    b. Describe what the product can do for the reader.
    c. Appeal to the emotions (love, goodness, joy); appeal to the rationality of the product or service (references to saving money, safety, convenience, etc. Use human nature appeals (to be well thought of, to be liked, etc.)
    d. Use as many paragraphs as you need for this section.

4. Proceed to the DESIRE section. The writer's job is to get the reader to really *want* the product or service. This section is written to reduce reader resistance and to convince the readers to purchase the product or service.
    a. Offer proof that what you are selling works.

b. Offer a guarantee.

c. Use a testimonial. What do others think about the product?

d. Use language that people will believe.

e. Introduce price strategically (show the price in small units, compare the price with your competitors, show how the reader is saving money by purchasing the product, make your price a bargain, show how the reader benefits by taking advantage of the price.)

f. Use as many paragraphs as you need in this section.

5. Stimulate ACTION. Get the reader to act. Use specific language to tell the reader what to do to get this product or service. Use one or more of the following suggestions:

a. Make the action as easy as possible. One short paragraph is usually sufficient for this section.

b. Supply the reader with an 800 telephone number.

c. Give the reader your web site address.

d. Offer an inducement or stimulus to get the reader to act quickly.

e. Set a specific date to act (Act *now*! Order *by May 10*. Sign your name on the attached card *today*.)

f. Use a postscript occasionally. A postscript stands out from the rest of the letter and tends to increase the chances for action from the reader.

ACTIVITIES

1. Bring a product from home in order to prepare a persuasive communication. Assume that you are preparing a sales letter that will go to over 100,000 people around the country. Study the product carefully; know to whom you are writing. Keep the letter to one page. Use the A-I-D-A approach.

2. Use the Internet to check information on writing a persuasive communication. Check to see what plans for gaining ATTENTION you can find. Check also to see what other ways to get ACTION exist. Use the information you have obtained to expand your ideas. Discuss your findings with other class members.

3. Use the A-I-D-A approach to prepare a one-page advertisement for the same product you used in #1 above. Include computer graphics; prepare your ad on a standard sheet of 8 ½ x 11-inch sheet of paper. Print the ad in color, if possible. Use the graphic capabilities to improve the

appearance of your ad; *e.g.,* italics, bolding, underlining, different sizes of type, etc.

4. Bring sample sales letters to class. Check your mail for examples of sales letters, or ask your friends and co-workers for samples they might give to you. Study the samples to see if they fit the A-I-D-A approach. Present your findings orally to the class.

5. Your sorority, fraternity, or club is interested in promoting a car wash this Saturday on the Commons at Central Michigan University. Cars will be washed for $5 each; the inside of the car will be cleaned for an additional $2. Write a persuasive sales letter that will be sent to all the clubs and organizations on the campus that will encourage their members to take advantage of the car wash. Sign the letter with your name as Project Director.

6. Use the information given in #5 above and prepare a one-page advertisement for posting on bulletin boards throughout the campus. Be creative.

RESOURCES

www.successfulminds.com: discusses how to write persuasive advertising copy and direct sales letters.

www.profitjump.com: discusses persuasive convincing as a valuable marketing tool.

www.marketingsource.com: gives shortcut ways to make sales letters more emotional.

www.geocities.com: discusses principles for advertisements and sales letters.

www.nineyards.com: provides ways to create a high-impact sales letter using persuasion.

✦ **Company Letterhead** ✦

January 1, 200x

Mr. Roberto Smith
12345 North Water Street
Kent, OH 44240

Dear Mr. Smith:

Are you tired of losing your pen? Do you ever run out of ink? If you answered yes to either of these questions, then read further!

With the new Giganto Pen, you will never run out of ink no matter where you are. Losing your pen will be impossible with the Giganto Pen. The Giganto's ink cartridges last up to five times as long as the average pen. And, because of its size, the pen is easy to find when you're ready to write.

Your pen comes in 20 different colors and can write in black, blue, red, and green ink. Ten extra cartridges are included with the initial order of the Giganto Pen. The pen may be large in size but weighs less than one ounce.

How much would you pay for your Giganto Pen: $10, $20, $30 or more? If you act now, you can get your Giganto Pen, along with a total of 20 cartridges, for only $5.99, a bargain you cannot refuse. The pen is guaranteed to your satisfaction; and, if you are unhappy with your pen **at any time**, return the Giganto for a full refund.

To get you Giganto Pen, call toll free 1-800-GIG-ANTO or email us at pen1@giganto **now**. If you act within the next 24 hours, we will include a **second pen** at no additional cost.

Sincerely,

Roger Lodger Dodger

Roger Lodger Dodger
Sales Director

| **TOPIC** | **Preparing a persuasive request** |

DEFINITION

A persuasive request will call on the ability to persuade someone to do something that he or she may or may not want to do or to persuade him or her to your point of view.

BACKGROUND

Use the same A-I-D-A approach you used to persuade someone to buy something. This time, however, you are making a persuasive request that does not include selling a product or a service.

STEPS

1. **Gain Attention.** Start with a compliment or a fact. Ask an interesting question. Tell the reader the benefits to expect. You may wish to start by asking the reader for help.

2. **Build Interest.** Prove the worth of your request by providing facts, figures, and details. Show how you can be of benefit to the reader.

3. **Reduce Resistance (Conviction, Desire).** Give counter arguments to possible obstacles. Know what you are talking about. Tell the receiver how he or she will benefit.

4. **Motivate Action.** Ask for specific action. Include an incentive. Set a date for action.

ACTIVITIES

1. As president of your local marketing group, the executive committee has decided to ask Rachel Collins, a well-known textbook author, to speak to the annual conference of your marketing group, Marketers for Americans. Provide dates, times, possible topics, and any other information Rachel will need to know. Anticipate what some of her objections or questions might be. Persuade Rachel Collins, the national president of Marketers for Americans, to speak at the conference. Write to Rachel at the following address:

   Ms. Rachel Collins
   324 West Hall
   Central Michigan University
   Mount Pleasant, MI 48859

2. As president of the Marketing Club at your school, you want to persuade the membership to take a field trip to an advertising agency in Chicago. You feel many benefits will be gained by all members. Write a persuasive memo to the Marketing Club that will convince them to sponsor the trip for all members.

3. The fraternities and sororities (Greeks) at your university are planning to put together a newsletter, published twice a semester, highlighting the events of the Greek community. In order to help with the costs of publication, you need to solicit the help of local businesses; you want them to advertise in your newsletter. Prepare a persuasive letter that can be used to convince local businesses to take out ads in your newsletter.

4. Identify a situation in your own life that requires you to write a persuasive request letter. Write and hand the letter in to your instructor.

5. Write a note to your "significant other" or another friend suggesting that you would like to have dinner this coming Saturday night at one of the classiest restaurants in town. Use your best persuasive style of writing.

RESOURCES

www.marketingsource.com: prepares readers to create a high-impact persuasive letter.

www.businessknowhow.com: discusses emotion for persuasion in sales letters or internal memos.

www.entrepreneur.com: talks about persuasion as a psychological tool; solid sales.

www.writeexpress.com: includes discussion of persuasive letters.

www.ducttapemarketing.com: tells how to write interesting and excellent persuasive letters.

www.soho.org: discusses creating high-impact persuasive letters.

Matilda Waters

waters1mk@cmich.edu
989.779.5555

789 Sterling Meadows
Mount Pleasant, MI 48858

November 23, 200x

Senator Henry Goodfellow
40 Senate Office Building
3987 North Michigan Avenue
Lansing, MI 43498

Dear Senator Goodfellow:

How would you like a bright, efficient young woman to intern in your office this summer?

As a political science student at Central Michigan University, I will receive a bachelor's degree a year from now. As an intern in your office, I would be able to handle correspondence from your constituents, run errands, answer the telephone and the email, and carry out other tasks that you ask me to do.

Although you haven't advertised for an intern, I have the feeling that if you find someone who will work efficiently, accurately, and intelligently, you would hire that person. I am that person, Senator Goodfellow.

After you have had time to study the enclosed up-to-date resume, please call me any day between 9 a.m. and 5 p.m. at (989) 555-8888 to schedule a time that I can meet with you.

Sincerely,

Matilda Waters

Matilda Waters

Enclosure

| TOPIC | Intercultural communication (written) |

Intercultural communication (written)

1. Appreciate the culture of other people instead of judging it. Stop ethnocentricity, the feeling that one's culture is superior to all other cultures. Demonstrate sensitivity to other cultures.

2. Avoid slang, idioms, jargon, redundancies, contractions, and clichés when writing to people in other countries.

3. Research the country before writing to someone in that country. The U.S. Post Office has helpful information about international mail practices that you can secure.

4. Try using the letter documentation of the country you are writing to. You can find this information at the U.S. Post Office as well. If you cannot find the correspondence documentation of another country, simply write in one of the formats with which you are familiar.

5. Use the *indirect* style in writing to people in high-context countries: Japan, China, and most Asian countries.

   a. Begin with a neutral statement. Talk about the weather, your family, and other nonbusiness issues.
   b. Provide details, facts, and explanation.
   c. State the objective or purpose of your communication. Tell why you are writing.
   d. Offer assistance. Close with a pleasant, forward-looking statement.

6. Use the *direct* style in writing to people in low-context countries (Germany, The Netherlands, and many European countries).

   a. State the objective or the purpose at the very beginning of the communication. Tell why you are writing.
   b. Provide details, facts, and explanation.
   c. Include a future-oriented final thought in a polite closing.

118

ACTIVITIES

1. Search the Internet and the library for information from at least ten countries on the nonverbal method of greeting that is used in that country. (Example: Japan uses a bow; the United States uses a firm handshake, etc.) Prepare a memo for your instructor. Discuss your findings in class.

2. Search the Internet and the library for information concerning international city and country telephone codes. Find the codes for at least 10 countries and cities. (Example: The telephone code for Egypt is 20; the telephone code for Cairo is 2).

3. Letter - Indirect Style. Write a letter to a Japanese businessman who plans to come to the United States for a three-week business meeting at your company. In his letter to you, he requested two connecting rooms on the first floor of the hotel. He needs a hotel with a swimming pool because he is bringing his three teenage children (2 boys and 1 girl) with him.

   In addition, he requests that the meetings he is to attend be held each day in the morning only—perhaps eight o'clock until noon. He wants to spend the time with his children in the afternoon.

   Also, he wants to know about vacation spots near Mount Pleasant that they all can visit in one day. He needs to be back for the meetings each morning. On the weekends, however, he would like a get-away with his children—somewhere they can stay for two nights and visit tourist attractions.

   Although his children are not of baby-sitting age, he would like someone to be with them in the mornings and when he is attending the meeting. Perhaps this someone could show the teenagers around town or attend nearby attractions. You are certain he wants his children to visit Central Michigan University as well as the parks, lakes, and picnic areas nearby.

   You feel that you are able to grant all of his requests. You had originally planned to have the business meeting for four hours a day—and the morning time is agreeable with you and your staff.

Write a letter to Motohiko-san in the indirect style.

> Sato Motohiko-san
> Toyohashi, Incorporated
> Go Toyohashi Macho
> Morikawa, Aichi Prefecture
> JAPAN 441

Note: Motohiko-san (a proper salutation)
Sayonara (goodbye—can be used as a complimentary closing)
Arigato (Thank you)
Domo arigato (Thank you very much)

4. Letter - Direct Style. You have been invited to give a presentation in Munich, Germany, on how business communication in the United States differs from business communication in Germany. Your audience will consist of employees from one of the larger companies in Munich, Autobahn Works Company.

You have a lot of information; you have studied all of the available travel folders and manuals, books on how to act abroad—especially in Germany—travel guides like the Fodor manuals, and other sources. In addition, you have talked with several people—one of whom lived in Germany for over 10 years—and two college students who spent a year abroad going to school in Munich. You felt that the information you have is going to be helpful.

You are to ask several questions about your presentation. How many people will be in attendance? How long should the presentation be? One hour? Two hours? Longer? Your main objective in this letter is to have your reader reserve a room for you at a hotel that is near to the place where you will be speaking. You need a large room, one that has PC facilities, fax, and plenty of workspace, since you plan to do a lot of work for your company while you are in Munich.   Write the letter in the direct style to the following person:

> Herr Karl Schroeder, Public Relations
> Autobahn Works Company
> Friedrichstrasse 498
> 87898 Munich
> GERMANY

Note: Very honorable Herr Schroeder (A salutation)
Auf Wiedersehen (Goodbye)
Danke (Thank you)
Bitte (Please)
Guten morgen (Good morning)

5. Use the Internet and the library to find typical working hours in the various countries. What time do workers usually begin? What time do workers usually end? Are any breaks permitted during the day? Write a short report to your instructor based on your findings. Research at least five different countries.

6. Use the Internet and the library to search to identify the characteristics that make up culture. What is culture? Where does culture come from? Parents? Friends? Location? Prepare a one- page memo to your instructor.

7. The following items can be used as a checklist for improving intercultural and international sensitivity. Use the Internet and the library to see how many additional items you can add to this list. Send a memo with a completed listing to your instructor.

    a. curb ethnocentrism
    b. speak and write in plain, simple English
    c. look beyond stereotypes
    d. encourage accurate feedback
    e. study your own culture

8. Place an **H** before the item that describes people from *high-context* cultures. Place and **L** before the item that describes people from *low-context* cultures. Check with your instructor for the correct answers or check your answers with the material in the text or from an Internet search.

    _____ action-oriented
    _____ may seem blunt or rude
    _____ tries to save face
    _____ group gets credit—not the individual
    _____ does not enjoy saying **no**
    _____ uses direct approach to communication
    _____ strong respect for rules and regulations

9. Use the Internet to find other characteristics of each type of culture. Prepare a complete listing of items and administer the list to another classmate.

10. Use the Internet and the library to prepare a list of telephone codes and numbers for the European countries. Explain how to make a telephone call to a company in one of the European countries. Consider the differences in time as one factor in placing a call. Present your findings orally to the class.

RESOURCES

http://www.andrews.edu/SBA/extension/BSAD560/HighLow.html discusses high- and low-context; strong interpersonal bonds, weak interpersonal bonds; high commitment and low commitment.

http://www.marin.cc.ca.us/buscom/index_page0008.htm: an anthropologist explains high- and low-context cultures.

http://www.visitseoul.net/english_new/seoul_world/world14.htm: a high context culture is discussed.

ASUMI TRADING COMPANY, LTD.

51 Morioka Machi
Moriyamaku, Nagoya 463 Japan

Motohiko Sato, President

November 15, 200x

Honorable Robert Goodman
Director of Sales
Mount Pleasant Recreational Games, Inc.
123245 Main Avenue
Mount Pleasant, MI 48858
U.S.A.

Allow us to open with reverence to you:

The spring season for cherry blossoms is here with us, and everybody is beginning to feel refreshed. We are all hoping that your family is well. We sincerely congratulate you on becoming more prosperous in your business. We hope that your winter is pleasant for you and for your family. You mentioned before that you like to ski. When will the weather in Michigan be available for skiing?

We have an inquiry from a foreign customer and shall be very happy to have your best price and technical literature for the Michigan Surf Board. Here are the questions for your kind reply:

- What is the size of the surfboard? Length? Weight? Width?
- What colors are available?
- Are surfboards only for adults? Do you have surfboards for children?
- What safety features are provided?
- What additional information can you supply?

The above are all the questions I have for this inquiry. Please give us the information necessary about these surfboards.

We shall be very pleased if you will study the inquiry and let us have your reply as soon as possible. We solicit your favor. Please give our regards and greetings to your family.

Let us close with great respect to you,

Fumitashi Matsui

Fumitashi Matsui
Director of Sales

BERLIN MOTOR WORKS

3498 Schroeder Strasse   **Berlin, Germany**

Herr Karl Weigland, Owner

November 14, 200x

Fraulein Christina Boehmer
Recreation, Inc.
334 West Global Avenue
Normal, IL 61987
U.S.A.

Very respected Ms. Christina Boehmer:

Please send me information about four passenger paddleboats that are available from Recreation, Inc. Specifically, I need the following information immediately:

- What colors are available?
- What is the minimum and maximum speed of the boat?
- Can two people paddle or just one?
- What are the various models you have available?
- What are the prices of the various models?
- Does the boat have a back-up gear as well as a forward gear?
- What are the safety features?
- What additional information can you send me?

I will be pleased if you study my inquiry and write me immediately.

Danke,

BERLIN MOTOR WORKS

Karl Weigland

Herr Karl Weigland
Owner

| **TOPIC** | **Email** |

DEFINITION   Email is an electronic memo and allows almost instantaneous, text-based messaging over the Internet. (See example on page 129.)

EXPLANATION   Email messages are prepared in a memo format with the standard memo headings already provided on your screen: TO, FROM, DATE, and SUBJECT.

1. Memos have always been reserved for internal communication within an organization only, but email has become widely accepted as a means of communication internally and externally.

2. Follow traditional memo format guidelines in creating an email message.
    a. Use block style and the direct pattern.
    b. Use paragraphs to organize your message.

KEY POINTS

1. Email has become one of the most preferred and most used channels of communication today.
    a. Email use saves time, money, and resources for businesses making email a valuable business tool.
    b. Business etiquette is different from informal; use correct capitalization, grammar, and punctuation. Avoid abbreviations and jargon.

2. A major concern when using email is "tone."
    a. Email is not considered the best communication method for creating relationships or for communicating emotions effectively.
    b. Email is most effective for sending the same message to many people, for communicating with individuals who are difficult to reach by phone, and as a convenient way to send an attachment.
    c. Email is most appropriate to use when you need to send a message that is not lengthy or complex and that does not involve confidential, sensitive, or emotional information.
    d. Do not use email to avoid direct contact or when discussion is needed.
    e. Do not email a business contact or customer unless you have been invited to do so.
    f. Never use all caps in Internet communications; all caps is equivalent to shouting.

3. Email is business correspondence; always maintain a professional tone.
   a. Compose your message with the same care as when preparing any other written business document; proofread carefully and spell check your message.
   b. Always include a subject line that identifies the purpose of your message.

4. If a response is required, be sure to state the fact clearly in your message.

5. When asked to respond, do so immediately.

6. If information is requested that will delay your response, send a brief message to inform the sender.

7. Be sure to refer to an attachment specifically within the message itself.

8. Do not include the original message in your reply.

9. Do not forward a message without permission.

10. Do not send personal emails on company time.

11. Email may not be the best way to communicate if you need an immediate response from people for a number of reasons:
    a. They do not use email or do not like to use email.
    b. They may not check their email regularly.
    c. They may be overwhelmed with email messages and yours is just one more.

12. Email provides a real threat to corporate security as the usage of email continues to increase.
    a. Do not send confidential or highly sensitive information through email; use the telephone or face-to-face meetings instead.

13. As with any written communication, email is a permanent document and can easily be saved and printed. Most importantly, an email message can easily be forwarded to anyone in a matter of seconds.
    a. Don't put anything in an email message you would not want anyone else to see!

14. Liability issues combined with employee abuse of email and Internet usage has resulted in the need to monitor employee usage. Be sure you follow the "acceptable usage policy" for your company regarding Internet usage to avoid losing your job!
    a. Many organizations have implemented Internet usage policies to cover all aspects of company email; such as, acceptable use, sending abusive email messages, email retention, company's right to monitor, access and security issues, software and system usage, personal use, appropriate Internet usage, copying or downloading copyrighted materials, no expectation of privacy on company network, and more.
    b. Many organizations monitor employee usage of email and the Internet as a means to enforce their Internet usage policy and to reduce their liabilities.

ACTIVITIES

1. In small groups, brainstorm to identify at least five advantages and five disadvantages of using email.

2. Conduct a class debate concerning Internet usage policies.
    a. Form teams for each side of the debate (organization vs. employees). To prepare, do some research to find examples of company Internet usage policies or check with local employers to find examples.
    b. Find news articles about current instances or lawsuits dealing with this issue.
    c. Consider what the pros and cons are for each side. What are the reasons for an organization to monitor employees and/or implement an Internet usage policy?
    d. What are the ethics and rights of the organization to the individual involved? Would you work for a company that did not allow you to send or receive personal email at work?

3. For each of the situations listed below, discuss whether email would be the best communication channel to use or not--and why:
    a. A new account representative needs to introduce herself to her 25 clients.
    b. Request information from a colleague who works in the overseas office.
    c. The time for a meeting has changed from tomorrow at 9:30 a.m. to 1:30 p.m.

127

d. Send a list of customers and account numbers to a colleague in a branch office.

e. Send the corporate phone directory to a new employee at his home office.

f. After a disagreement in a meeting with a colleague, you want to communicate your regrets for any hard feelings.

4. Bring a copy of a company's "acceptable usage policy" to class to discuss. You can find them on the Internet, ask someone for their company's, or bring in your own employer's. Find news articles about recent cases involving the termination of employment based on a breach of such policies by employees.

"Cc" means carbon copy – include email address of other(s) you need to send a copy of the message to

Email program provides memo headings automatically, including date; don't include these headings again in your message

From: Robert Thompson
Sent: Wed 8/11/2004 2:33 PM
To: Todd Smart
Cc:
Subject: Program revisions

Include salutation when message is sent outside the company

Use block format style - double space between paragraphs; single space within paragraphs

Dear Todd:

We have just completed the program revisions you requested. We were able to keep the information you prepared in the format you desired for the primary document and still stay within the page number limitations. The final documentation will be sent to you when we receive your reply to this message.

We hope you are satisfied with the work we have completed and look forward to doing business with you again in the near future. It has been our pleasure to serve you.

Sincerely,

Robert Thompson

Use a complimentary closing and include your name when a salutation is used

Always request a reply if required and deadline if appropriate

| TOPIC | Netiquette |

| DEFINITION | Use of proper and acceptable practices when communicating on the Internet, including using email and especially for business-related purposes, is called "netiquette." |

| EXPLANATION | Knowing and following proper netiquette is important. Conventions for acceptable usage and formatting guidelines continue to develop for the use of email, discussion lists, and other forms of Internet communication. |

KEY POINTS

1. Internet communication such as email and discussion boards are typically instantaneous. Don't forget to consider how your remarks may or may not be interpreted by others. When sound and body language is absent, text alone can be misconstrued. Humor is often lost in the transmission and can be easily misinterpreted.

2. If in a discussion list, stick to the subject. Look at what others have already said before you post to avoid repeating something just discussed. Review archives as well.

3. Do not make statements that could be interpreted as an official representation of your employer or as offers to do business.

4. Never be rude or inflame someone (known as "flaming"). Flame wars can create serious problems such as receiving unwanted mail and cluttering mailboxes.

5. Don't type anything you wouldn't tell someone face-to-face." Someone can easily forward your communication to others, print it, or show it to others without your consent.

6. Do not send or forward "jam" junk email to someone you know (jokes, chain letters, etc.)

7. As explained previously, don't use all caps (the equivalent of cyber shouting), always fill in the subject line, and be sure your reply refers to the subject.

8. Avoid password security problems. When a web site asks if you want them to "remember" your password for future visits, say "NO!" Email scams use a common name as the sender (like "John" or "Bob") to make you think the writer is someone

you know. Access to your online account is gained when you try to open an attachment, giving the writer your credit card information.

1. Prepare a memo to all employees about the importance of netiquette in the workplace. Include the at least three specific netiquette issues your company wants all employees to be informed of. Refer employees to at least one Internet web site you feel will provide them with further information on netiquette.

2. Find a copy of a company's acceptable usage policy (as discussed on page 127) and see what points in their policy may or may not relate to netiquette. Discuss improvements or potential loop holes that may exist in the company's policy as it relates to netiquette.

| **TOPIC** | **Cell phone etiquette** |

EXPLANATION

The lack of respect for others due to the improper use of cell phones in public has led to the need for cell phone etiquette. Rules for the courteous use of cell phones are being developed and publicized to promote good manners for cell phone usage and to avoid over exposure to "second-hand conversations."

Knowing and following proper cell phone etiquette is important. Conventions for proper use of cell phones continue to develop. Every business person who relies on their cell phone needs to know and practice cell phone etiquette.

KEY POINTS

1. Respect the rules when asked or posted in an establishment to turn off cell phones. Turning your cell phone on vibrate is not acceptable in situations where cell phones can interfere with other equipment such as on airplanes and in hospitals.

2. Don't infringe on others' personal space, both physical proximity and sound. Be mindful of how close you are to others when using your cell phone in a public place and lower your voice. You may not think you're talking loudly on your phone; but if everyone around you can hear you, you're invading their personal space.

3. Don't talk on the cell phone when in the company of others. If you must take the call, tell the caller you will call them back and end the call immediately. Be sure to apologize for the interruption. When necessary to take a call, excuse yourself from the presence of others and make the conversation brief. Carrying on a cell phone conversation while others have to listen and/or wait for you to finish is rude and unprofessional.

4. When alone in a restaurant, follow the lead of others. If no one is using a cell phone, then the use of the cell phone is likely to be frowned upon. Some restaurants cater to business people, and the use of cell phones by diners is much more acceptable.

5. Some situations occur where you simply should not bring your cell phone... funerals, weddings, church services, and a job interview are a few examples.

6. Don't set your cell phone to an annoying, elaborate ring tone, or, worse yet, a melody that rings continuously until answered. These elaborate "rings" are perceived as juvenile and unprofessional; the noise pollution is unnecessary. What might be a cute ring tone around your friends is not going to impress your boss or clients.

ACTIVITIES

1. As a class or in groups, make a list of bad cell phone manners you have witnessed or committed yourself. Once your list is completed, discuss each "infraction" and identify what should have been done. Are there instances where cell phone etiquette is different for personal versus business situations?

2. See if your cell phone manners are up to speed. Take the cell phone etiquette quiz at the following web site: http://tech.monster.com/articles/clellphone/

RESOURCES

Check out these web sites on cell phone etiquette:

www.cellmanners.com

www.letstalk.com/promo/unclecell/unclecell2.htm

www.cnn.com/2003/TECH/10/29/hln.wired.cell.etiquette/

TOPIC	**Preparing reports**

TYPES

Informational reports are those reports that provide information only. Usually no analysis of the data is given.

Analytical reports analyze the data presented, and the writer should give conclusions and recommendations.

BACKGROUND

Information provided in a report will help the busy executive or busy employee make a more informed decision on a particular project or area of study. Most companies are trying to curtail the length of reports because most people just do not have the time necessary to read a long report. Once in a while, however, you may need to prepare a long report due to the subject matter of the report.

KEY POINTS

1. Organize the report into a standard report format. Your company may have a company manual that gives an accepted format for preparing reports.

2. Write the Introduction. The introduction to a report contains some or all of the following parts:

    a. Authorization and Background. Usually at the beginning of the report you will have a short section that gives a little background about the report; namely, who authorized the report, why the report was completed, and who was involved in completing the report.

    b. The Problem Statement. The first item that should appear is the problem statement. What is the topic of the paper? What are you writing about? The statement of the problem should be directly to the point.

    c. Purpose of the Report. Why did you prepare this report?

    d. Scope and Analysis. What is covered in the report? What is not covered in the report?

    e. Delimitations. What controls have you, the writer, placed on the subject? A report cannot cover every detail of every explanation. What have you decided to include in the report?

134

f. Limitations. What factors do you not have control of in this study? What factors are inherent in the study itself?

g. Preliminary Pages. After the report has been completed, you may wish to add a cover or title page.

h. Memo of Transmittal. On the top of the report, include a memo that transmits the report to the person or persons for whom you prepared the report. Business people have many projects being carried out simultaneously. A memo of transmittal will recall the original project for the reader.

i. Executive Summary. If the report is lengthy (over three pages), prepare an executive summary of the report so that the gist of the report can be understood quickly.

RESOURCES

http://owl.english.purdue.edu/workshops/hypertext/reportw/ - information on many aspects of writing research reports.

www.msugf.edu - guides for APA style.

www.enchantedlearning.com - includes topics and rubrics for writing a research report.

http://www.ccc.commnet.edu/mla/index.shtml - includes guidelines for research papers based on APA style.

www.ipl.org - the Internet Public Library; provides help in finding ideas for what to read before writing the research paper.

TO:

FROM:

DATE:

SUBJECT:

> TS before first paragraph

> Use bullets or numbers for reporting brief points or use paragraphs for each point if needed.

Include a brief statement that introduces your topic.

- *Discuss first point you're reporting on.*

- *Discuss second point, etc.*

Provide concluding remarks in last paragraph.

> Key point: An informational report provides information only with no analysis or interpretation provided.

TO: Dan Hemsfield

FROM: Mary Tofston *MT*

DATE: September 18, 200x

SUBJECT: Survey results on the Fab 2000

Triple space before first paragraph and before headings

We have completed our survey on our new vacuum cleaner, the Fab 2000. The following section reports our findings and analyses of the survey results related to consumer response to the Fab 2000 Model.

Recommendations

To improve the potential sales of the Fab 2000, we recommend the following changes be made prior to market release:

- Prepare a more detailed owner's manual that includes pictures of each component.

- Reduce the retail price to better compete with the Hoover XLR model.

Findings and Analyses

The preliminary assessment of the survey data found the Fab 2000 well received by consumers. The new features of this model appear to make the model very attractive to consumers over the nearest competition.

The overall design of the Fab 2000 was also appealing to consumers. However, a common concern was whether the cord would hold up with heavy use.

The majority of consumers responded favorably to all categories on the survey concerning convenience, ease of use, design, and suction power.

TOPIC   **Progress (interim) report**

DEFINITION   A progress report is prepared periodically giving the status of a report or a project.

BACKGROUND   If you are working on a project, your supervisor needs to know what has been accomplished to date and what remains to be completed.

KEY POINTS

1. **Introduction**. The introduction to a progress report contains a brief statement of the purpose, overview, background, and nature of the project. Because your supervisor may have many projects going at the same time from many different individuals or teams, he or she will appreciate knowing the exact title and description of the project.

2. **Work completed.** The work completed section provides all pertinent information about the present status of the project, including:

   a. A summary of the work finished during prior reporting periods.
   b. A summary of the work finished since the last report.

3. **Work yet to complete.** This section is an overview of the remaining work to be done on the project, with target dates. An estimate of the final deadline date appears in this section.

4. **Conclusion.** The concluding section of a progress report is used to bring certain information about the goals of the project to the attention of the person authorizing the work. The conclusion might, for example, explain current or projected delays or cost overruns so that, if necessary, the reader can anticipate or make contingency plans.

STEPS

1. Use memo format to prepare a progress report. Indicate the TO, FROM, DATE, and SUBJECT.

2. Keep the progress report short. Rarely will you have a report more than one page.

3. Send a copy of the progress report to your supervisor and to any one else involved in the writing of the report.

1. Prepare a progress report for a task you are working on in this class or another class.

2. Prepare a progress report in memo format on your status as a student at this university. Write a short introduction; state the work you have completed; tell what has yet to be completed before you graduate from the university, and give the date you expect to graduate.

3. Prepare a progress report for a project you worked on in an internship or in a summer job.

4. Choose one of the classes you are taking this semester. Write a short paper citing your progress so far in the class. Submit the report in a memo to your instructor.

RESOURCES

http://www.io.com/~hcexres/tcm1603/acchtml/progrep.html - explains progress reports, how to prepare, and gives an example.

http://owl.english.purdue.edu/ - information on all types of writing.

TO: Tom Slick

FROM: Amy Downing, *AD* Mike Feeney, ᴍꜰ Laura Shumaker *LS*

DATE: March 27, 200x

SUBJECT: Progress Report for Training Session

Introduction: The need for our employees to conduct business abroad has led to the training development initiative. The progress of our research and planning for the employee training session on cultural sensitivity is as follows:

 We are preparing an employee training session to improve employees' knowledge of other cultures. Our goal is to improve employees' awareness of business practices and cultural differences in other countries as a result of this training experience. We have developed a time line outlining the major goals and objectives, including the dates we expect to complete each goal or objective.

Work Completed: We have completed a survey of employees to determine their current knowledge related to cultural sensitivity issues. We have developed a preliminary outline of the training session, including the major topics to be included based on the results of our survey. We are also designing activities that will make the training session interactive while reinforcing the information.

Work Yet to Complete: We are in the process of gathering the materials and resources to include in the training session. The materials and resources should be gathered by April 1. Our next goal is to prepare the necessary promotional material by April 5 to distribute to employees, informing them of the training session.

Anticipated Problems: At this time, we do not anticipate any problems in completing the training session on time. We expect to be prepared to conduct the training session, as planned, on April 15.

TOPIC   **Executive summary**

DEFINITION   An executive summary is a condensed report summarizing concisely the contents and perspective of a longer document. An executive summary is also used to summarize the contents of an oral presentation.

BACKGROUND   An executive summary serves two functions: (1) the executive summary may be used as a condensed version taking the place of the original document or presentation, or (2) the executive summary may serve to introduce the important features of a longer document that will be read on another occasion.

KEY POINTS

1. Study the original document carefully. Determine the items you feel are most important and that are representative of the original document.

2. Summarize the contents of the material into a few precise paragraphs that will serve as a reliable summary for another reader. Avoid stating opinions or your thoughts. The paper is a summary, not a critical review.

3. Format the executive summary using block or modified block style.

4. Give a complete citation at the top of the page. There are web sites that provide information on formatting guidelines for the major style guides (such as APA and MLA). Refer to the web site sources listed on the following page.

5. Be sure to include the date; the name of the person who prepared the summary also appears at the top of the page.

6. Single-space the paragraphs, but double space between them.

7. The length of the executive summary depends upon the original presentation or article. An executive summary is roughly 10 percent of the original document or presentation.

ACTIVITIES

1. Find a two- or three-page article in a current popular news or financial magazine such as *Time, Newsweek, U.S. News and World Report,* or *Fortune.* Prepare an executive summary of the article to turn in with a copy of the original article attached.

2. Write an executive summary for a lecture on campus or a guest speaker you heard in a class.

3. Watch a news show or listen to a speaker on the television. Prepare an executive summary of the presentation.

4. Write an executive summary of one of your instructor's classroom presentations. Give your instructor a copy of your summary.

5. Write an executive summary of a nonbusinesss article you have read recently. If you have a copy of the article, attach the article to the summary.

6. Write a summary in executive style of a movie or television show you have seen lately. Select two people—one who has seen the movie or television show and one who has not seen the movie nor the television show—and have them read your summary. Compare the differences in the two summaries. Note the differences in the responses. Decide whether your summary was detailed enough.

RESOURCES

Style guides for citations, writing papers, etc.

www.apastyle.org/ - APA style guide, includes guidelines for electronic sources.

http://owl.english.purdue.edu/handouts/research/r_apa.html - APA style guide from Purdue University online writing lab (OWL).

http://owl.english.purdue.edu/handouts/research/r_mla.html?PickLink=http://owl.english.purdue.edu/handouts/research/r_mla.html - MLA style guide from Purdue University OWL.

Executive summaries

http://www.columbia.edu/~ftg1/WRITING%20EXECUT.SUMMARY.html - explains how to write an executive summaries and what elements to include.

www.writing-skills.com - details tips for writing executive summaries.

EXECUTIVE SUMMARY
by
Your Name
Current Date

Morales, Lourdes. "Great Times at Feather, Inc., All the Time," *Business Weekly News,* January 31, 200x, pp. 14-17.

Currently, Feather, Inc., located in Mount Pleasant, Michigan, is looking to expand the company's horizons. The Marketing Research Division recently conducted a research study to find whether locating a branch of the company in Germany would be beneficial to the parent company.

Through extensive research, the division reached the conclusion that Germany would not be able to support the current market line due to cultural factors, location of the plant, language barriers, poor climate, high liability, and a bleak outlook for available employees.

Recommendations made to the President and CEO of Feather, Inc., are the following: (1) keep looking for a suitable site in Europe; (2) watch the European economy for any signs of improvement; and (3) consider establishing an additional plant in the southern part of the United States.

| **TOPIC** | **Writing instructions for employees** |

DEFINITION　Instructions are written for the use of products, procedures, and for giving directions to employees.

EXPLANATION　Guidelines for writing instructions are usually included in the company employee manual. Instructions include the basic rules of writing and are divided into three sections: an introduction, a body, and a closing.

KEY POINTS

1. **The introduction.** The introduction to any instructions should provide basic information about the product or service or task and should answer the questions, who, what, when, where, why, and how.

2. **The body.** Write the actual directions you want the reader to follow in the order you want those directions followed.

    a. The first word of every numbered instruction should begin with an *active* verb; such as, *gather, place, pull, turn, remove, flip, start, stop, turn.*

    b. Finish the instruction with additional sentences; these sentences can use an active or nonactive verb.

    c. Instructions should be understandable by all who read them. Short, concise sentences help readability. Long, complicated words, terms, and phrases that are not easily understood by everyone should be avoided.

    d. Include a warning or caution if needed. Think of ways the users could harm themselves in the use of the product or service.

3. **The closing.** Close with a separate paragraph. Give some encouragement to the reader for following these instructions (*e.g.,* If you follow these instructions, you should have many years of use from your new blender.")

1. Write instructions for one of the following office tasks: (a) how to give CPR in the office; (b) what to do in case of a disaster, such as an earthquake, fire, or explosion; (c) how to fax a document; (d) how to use proper procedures for recycling; or (e) what tips to use for reducing stress in the office.

2. Use the Internet and the library to find a list of "active" verbs. Cite the web site. Send a list of at least 50 active verbs to your instructor in memo format.

3. Write instructions for a task that you select.

4. Write instructions for playing the card game "Fish" or "Crazy Eights" or another card game you know. Form teams of card players who will follow *exactly* the written instructions. After the game is over, allow each of the team members to offer suggestions as to how the instructions could be written to make them clearer. Each team should re-write the instructions—then all teams play the game again using their own re-written rules.

5. Bring a product and a list of instructions that detail the use of a small appliance. Choose someone from the class to read the instructions and use the appliance in front of the rest of the class. Are the instructions easy to follow? What suggestions can the class members make that would make the instructions clearer? Discuss.

6. Write instructions for giving CPR to a person who just fainted in your office or who is choking on food.

RESOURCES

http://www.io.com/~hcexres/tcm1603/acchtml/instrux.html - explains the technical writing process.

http://www.techscribe.co.uk/techw/business_writing_samples.htm - explains how to write instructions in the world of work.

INSTRUCTIONS FOR MOST EFFICIENT USE
OF COFFEE BREAKS
AT XYZ CORPORATION

Employees are offered two coffee breaks of 15 minutes each—one break in the morning and the other in the afternoon. The following are to serve as guidelines for coffee breaks:

1. **Set a specific time.** Before arriving at work, schedule two break times. Make sure one break is in the morning and the other in the afternoon.

2. **Set your watch to a work clock.** Make sure that your watch reads the same time as your work clock does.

3. **Look at the clock.** Be aware of the time and how long you have until your break starts. **Warning:** If you leave the building, a greater risk occurs that you will not arrive back in time; others may report you for doing so.

4. **Take your break.** When the designated time has arrived, you may leave. As you are leaving, tell a colleague that you are going on break. In this way, you will not be abusing your coffee break.

5. **Look at the clock.** Make sure you look at your clock while you are on break so you know how much time you have left.

6. **Start to work.** When your break is over, you should start working again. Utilize the same process for the afternoon break.

Two coffee breaks are given to each employee twice a day. These privileges can be lost if employees abuse their privileges. Follow the above steps to ensure your freedom and relaxation during working hours.

Preparing a press release

A press release is an announcement sent to the media relating something that is taking place in your company that you want everyone to know.

BACKGROUND A press release must be clear and concise and should be written with particular attention to the five w's and the one h: who, what, where, when, why, and how. Write the press release so that the most important item is first, the second most important item second, and so on until the release is finished. This type of writing is called the *Inverted Pyramid Style*. The Inverted Pyramid style of writing provides the essence of the story first and adds details in a descending order of importance.

Also, if a newspaper has limited space for the story, the editor will cut the story *starting from the **bottom** paragraph and working upwards until the story fits the space available.* Limit the document to one or two double-spaced pages. Be credible—have no typos, no misspelled words, and no factual errors.

STEPS

1. Use letterhead paper with two-inch right and left margins.

2. Use double spacing.

3. Indent each paragraph.

4. Leave the top one-third of the page blank for the editors to use.

5. Indicate when the material is to be released.

6. Provide a name and number for the editor so that he or she may call you for clarification or for additional material.

7. Begin with the place and date of the announcement. Usually the date line (city, state, and date) is placed in all capital letters at the start of the announcement.

8. Keep paragraphs to one sentence only.

9. Type MORE a double space down from the last line on all pages (except the last) if the release is longer than one page.

10. Type the page number at the top left on the second and subsequent pages four times with a hyphen between each

number (see examples of press releases pages 151-154) so that attention is called to the page.

11. Type a shortened title or description of what the article is about at the right side of the second and subsequent pages.

12. Type END and double space down from the last line of the article.

ACTIVITIES

1. Prepare a press release for a fictitious company that announces plans for a new building in downtown Mount Pleasant. The following facts, in no special order, should be used in the press release:

   a. new office building in downtown Mount Pleasant
   b. five stories—every office looks out on the city park
   c. purchased from three local businesspersons: Able Cain, Mabel Virgo, and Consuelo Schultz
   d. 16,000 square feet of office space
   e. purchased for $143 million
   f. 50 assigned parking spaces; 100 spaces for visitors
   g. walls and partitions are flexible and can be arranged in a variety of ways
   h. will accommodate company's expanding executive force—due to increase in sales
   i. sales have increased 73 percent in the last decade
   j. three sets of restrooms included on each floor
   k. building is accessible to all—physically challenged, etc.
   l. kitchen and dining area on each floor
   m. a "resting" lounge on each floor—contains books for reading, TV, stereo, reclining chairs; coffee and donuts provided daily
   n. auditorium for conferences and seminars will seat up to 500

   Use the Inverted Pyramid Style of Writing. Remember to put the *most important* item in the first paragraph. Then put the *next most important* item in the next paragraph and so on until the final paragraph contains the *least important* item.

   The reason for this type of writing procedure is that some newspapers will not have space for the entire story you submitted. In order to get the story to fit in the space available, the editor will cut the story, beginning from the bottom paragraph and moving up. So, that is the reason you need to put the most important items at the beginning of the story.

The press release is from you, the head of the public relations department, and should be marked for immediate release. See the two examples of press releases beginning on page 151.

2. Write a press release that announces that YOU are the new sales director for ABCD Corporation. You will start at the beginning of next month. Provide interesting facts and information. Include all the necessary details and write the story in the Inverted Pyramid Style. Again, check out the examples beginning on page 151.

3. Write a story about one of your friends who has received the honor of being the first person in his family to complete a college education. Find some interesting facts about the person, and include those facts in the story. The story will be featured in the Sunday edition of the *Morning Sun* as a feature article. Check your final copy with the format given beginning on page 151.

4. Find a press release of a company in one of the local newspapers. Study the article carefully. What do you see as the differences in that article compared to the standards and principles used in this section of the text? Write a memo to your instructor. Attach a copy of the article you found.

5. Write a press release for the local newspaper announcing that your company is now smoke-free. No smoking is permitted within 100 feet of the building.

RESOURCES

www.press-release-writing.com - provides ten essential tips on writing effective press releases.

www.entrepreneur.com - goes beyond the press release into a public-relations plan.

Prepare the *lead* (the first part of news story that provides the most important facts of the story in the fewest words possible.) The lead should answer the following questions:

- *Who* was involved?
- *What* happened?
- *When* did it happen?
- *Where* did it happen?
- *Why* did it happen?
- *How* did it happen?

These questions are the ones that the reader wants answered immediately. An effective news story will answer all six questions if they are answerable at the time when the story breaks.

Another requirement of the lead is the *attribution statement,* usually placed at the end of the lead. The attribution tells the reader where the information came from. Note the following example of a lead that utilizes the who, what, when, where, why, and how, along with the attribution statement:

*A young man (**who**) was fatally injured (**what**)* Saturday evening (**when**) at the intersection of Maple and Elm streets (**where**) as his car entered the intersection (**how**) as a young boy broke loose from his mother's hand and ran in front of the car, (**why**) according to a police officer. (**attribution statement**)

(Then complete the remainder of the story with all the information at your disposal.)

John Foster, 28, of 2345 Main Avenue, Mount Pleasant, died Saturday evening at the corner of Maple and Elm Streets when he swerved to miss Joey Heatherford, the three-year-old son of Josh and Maria Heatherford of 153 North Oak Boulevard. Foster missed the boy, who had run from his mother's grasp. Foster's car skidded into a telephone poll, fatally injuring him. Officers said that Foster was dead instantly at the scene. Joey Heatherford was not injured. Foster, employed at ABCD Corporation since 2001, is survived by his wife of five years, Emily, a daughter, Amelia, 3, and a son, Eric, 18 months. Funeral arrangements are pending.

In press release format, the story may appear as follows:

Example 1 – Press Release

ABCD CORPORATION

12345 Main Avenue   Mount Pleasant, MI 48858

FOR IMMEDIATE RELEASE

For additional information, call:

Martin Leblanc, Publicity
(989) 777-7777

MOUNT PLEASANT, MICHIGAN, AUGUST 1, 200x. A

young man was fatally injured Saturday evening at the inter-

section of Maple and Elm Streets as his car entered the inter-

section when a young boy broke loose from his mother's hand

and ran in front of the car, according to a police officer.

John Foster, 28, of 2346 Main Avenue, Mount Pleasant, died

Saturday evening at the corner of Maple and Elm Streets when he

MORE

swerved to miss Joey Heatherford, the three-year-old son of Josh and

Maria Heatherford of 153 North Oak Boulevard.

Foster swerved and missed the boy, who had run

from his mother's grasp.

Foster's car skidded into a telephone poll, fatally injuring

him.

Officers said that Foster was dead instantly at the scene.

Joey Heatherford was not injured.

Foster, an employee of ABCD Corporation since

2001, is survived by his wife, Emily, of five years and by

his daughter, Amelia, 3, and his son, Eric, 18 months.

END

Example 2 - Press Release

ABCD CORPORATION

12345 Main Avenue   Mount Pleasant, MI 48858

Leave 2-3 inches between
letterhead and first line to
allow room for editor to
make comments, changes,
and suggestions

FOR IMMEDIATE RELEASE

For additional information, call:

Martin Leblanc, Publicity
(989) 777-7777

MOUNT PLEASANT, MICHIGAN, AUGUST 1, 200x.

ABCD Enterprises, Inc., has come up with a new idea for

the children of employees to manage their college loans.

According to recent estimates made by the Human

Resources Department at ABCD Enterprises, Inc., the typical

student, graduates with approximately $20,000 in federal loans.

MORE

ABCD suggests that stretching out the payments while lowering the interest rate can give the borrower enough room to avoid down credit-card bills that do not promote savings.

Consolidating expenses early can help lower the time to pay back the loans quickly and safely.

Those persons who want to take advantage of this plan or who want to hear more information about the plan should call the ABCD Enterprises, Inc., offices at (999-9999) as soon as possible.

ABCD Enterprises, Inc., has been in Mount Pleasant, Michigan, since 1955.

Over 500 people are employed in the Mount Pleasant plant.

ABCD has five branch offices around the country in major locations: Baltimore, Maryland; Chicago, Illinois; Bangor, Maine; Deerfield Beach, Florida; and Santa Fe, New Mexico.

The president of ABCD Enterprises, Inc., is Marylou Beatty, who has been with the company for over 11 years. She was formerly CEO of Ballistics Products.

END

TOPIC   # Writing a proposal

DEFINITION   A business proposal is a plan of intent to fill a need. Proposals can cover almost any subject and are either *solicited,* submitted in response to a written announcement or request for proposal (RFP), or *unsolicited,* proposals that sell a service or product to an individual or an organization that has not requested a proposal. Proposals tell a person, group, or agency what you will do, when you will do it, and how much it will cost in terms of time and resources.

BACKGROUND   The writer of a proposal tries to show that the proposal, if implemented, will lead to the solving a need or problem for the business. Answer these questions before you begin the proposal:

a. What is the subject of the proposal?
b. For whom is the proposal intended?
c. How do you intend the proposal to be used?
d. What is the deadline date for submission of the proposal and for tentative implementation of the proposed solution?
e. Have you reviewed the literature on the Internet and in the library that will provide support for your proposal? How have other companies handled similar situations?

STEPS

1. The introduction presents and summarizes the background for the proposal? Who authorized the proposal? Your supervisor? Your department head? The CEO? Identify your readers. Did you come up with the idea on your own? Who is the audience for your proposal? Will your proposal be presented only in writing, or will you be asked to present the proposal orally?

2. State what you propose to do. What is the proposal about? What do you want to see happen within the company, within your department, within your office? What is your overall plan?

3. Provide the scope of the proposal. What do you plan to include? What will you *not* include? How will you restrict the proposal (delimitations)? What restrictions may occur that are not under your control (limitations)?

4. Gather the information necessary to complete the proposal? Do you need to prepare and send out a questionnaire to the other employees to get their opinions? Do you need to visit the library or the Internet to gather any kind of information needed to prepare your proposal?

5. Prepare a work schedule and project a time limit. When do you think you will finish the project? Prepare a listing of target dates; for instance, you may wish to break down the time periods into one- or two-week sessions. Your boss may ask you for periodic progress reports until the proposal is finished.

6. Prepare a list of resources needed; such as, money, equipment, additional help? Do you need time away from your job to complete the proposal? What else do you need?

7. Request approval. After you have prepared the proposal, ask for approval to go ahead and do what you have proposed to do.

ACTIVITIES

1. Using one of the following situations, prepare an organizational proposal. Use the material you just read to prepare the proposal. You may assume that you have been asked to prepare a proposal (solicited) or that you have come up with an idea of your own (unsolicited). See the sample proposal at the end of this section.

   a. a drug testing and drug awareness program for your company
   b. a childcare program for all employees
   c. three new PC's for your department
   d. an up-to-date web page for your employees
   e. in-house training program for all employees regarding any one of the following workplace issues:
      1) sexual harassment
      2) attendance at company-sponsored events
      3) a no-smoking policy within the building
      4) a day-care facility for all employees

2. Prepare a second proposal. Use one of the ideas mentioned in #1 above or, with the approval of your instructor, come up with an idea of your own.

3. Search the Internet or go to the library to see what other information you can find about *internal* and *external*

proposals. Also, read more about *solicited proposals, unsolicited proposals,* and *RFP (request for proposal).* Send your instructor a short memo of your findings.

4.   Identify the following proposal terms: investigative proposal, organizational proposal, and product proposal. Prepare a short memo of your findings for your instructor.

5.   Investigate two of the web site sources listed below. Prepare and submit to your instructor a short memo summarizing the web sites.

RESOURCES

http://www.learnerassociates.net/proposal/ - prepares students and others to learn more about the actual proposal writing process.

http://www.gpc.edu/~ebrown/pracguid.htm - tells how to produce a good proposal step by step.

www.nonprofits.org - tells how to get started writing a proposal.

http://www.slu.edu/research/proposal_development_toolkit .html - explains the research necessary prior to writing the proposal.

www.theresearchassistant.com - takes students through a tutorial for writing a proposal.

WXYZ CORPORATION

Interoffice Memorandum

TO: Claudia L. Finch, Supervisor, Projects Department

FROM: Alonzo Evening, Project Director AE

               Sandy Beech, Assistant Project Director SB

DATE: October 15, 200x

SUBJECT: Proposal for Globalization Options

Attached is a proposal for globalization options for WXYZ Corporation. Our team has researched the topic and feels that we can conduct the study for our company. The following information will help you determine whether or not completing the study is feasible.

The Project

WXYZ is interested in expanding its operations—either in this country or overseas. Currently, the division feels that Switzerland would be a compatible international market place for products from our company. Therefore, a study of the culture and the economy of Switzerland to determine if that country is a viable option for this move will be undertaken.

Authorization and Background

Earlier this month, you mentioned that our company was exploring globalization options and that those who wanted to take part in presenting a proposal are asked to do so. We as project directors of the company want to take part in the project. This proposal is submitted in response to your request.

Purpose

The purpose is to investigate, through both primary and secondary research, the feasibility of Switzerland as an international outlet for WXYZ Corporation. A further purpose of this proposal is to make information available to WXYZ management so that they will be able to decide on whether or not to expand into Switzerland.

Scope

To determine if WXYZ Corporation should take steps to locate an international outlet within the borders of Switzerland, the following questions must be answered:

1. Would the Swiss culture be open to an American toy manufacturer producing products in Switzerland?

2. Is the Swiss economy strong enough to support a recreational products manufacturer?

3. Would our products be acceptable in their culture?

4. What are the cultural norms of Switzerland pertaining to business socialization?

Delimitations

The study will be confined to research conducted on the Swiss culture. This research will be conducted using library information, Internet sources, and personal contact with members of that culture.

Limitations

The sources obtained may not adequately convey how the culture realistically functions as a whole. Depending on which part of the country from which the sources are gathered, different views may exist. Therefore, the views and opinions should serve as a preliminary guideline to determine if further research should be conducted of other sectors of the population.

Methodology

Data Collection. Primary data will be obtained through research conducted electronically as well as personal interviews with knowledgeable persons. Each project director of each team will be responsible for collecting the data. Secondary sources from the library and from the Internet will be used whenever feasible.

Data Analysis. These data will be used to determine whether a move to Switzerland will be appropriate at this time. The information will be evaluated on a subjective basis.

Data Presentation. The project directors will submit the findings, conclusions, and recommendations to the supervisor of the project. In addition, the supervisor will receive a progress report approximately every two weeks. The final report will be compiled into a presentation format, which will be presented to employees of WXYZ Corporation during the early part of December.

Project Time Line

Since the project directors have other responsibilities while working on this project, approximately three weeks will be needed to complete the study. The estimated time to complete the entire project is 40 hours. The following is a schedule of targeted dates:

Conduct research	November 1, 200x
Analyze data	November 15, 200x
Complete the report	November 20, 200x
Presentation of findings	December 1, 200x

Resources Needed

The project directors will use an average of 20 hours to conduct the research and 20 hours to analyze and interpret the data. The cost of supplies is due to long-distance charges stemming from international communication with Swiss residents and officials. The remaining time will be devoted to determining the best way to present the data to the employees. Currently, a written report and a PowerPoint presentation are anticipated. Total estimated cost is $15,500.

Additional help	$6,000
Phone expenses	$5,000
Miscellaneous	$4,500
TOTAL	$15,500

Request for Approval

Your approval of this proposal by October 25, 200x, will permit the project to begin and end according to the above schedule. If you have any questions regarding the proposal, please call or email either or both of us. Your reply is eagerly anticipated.

| **TOPIC** | **Preparing a code of ethics** |

DEFINITION

A code of ethics sets the ethical climate for an organization. A code of ethics sets a standard for correct and honest behavior and tells how ethical issues will be handled within the organization.

BACKGROUND

Management must encourage ethical awareness in their organizations from the top to the bottom. Many companies provide training programs to increase sensitivity to ethical issues.

KEY POINTS

Qualities of ethical behavior in business consist of the following characteristics or traits:

1. **Honesty and Integrity.** Employees must be truthful, frank, and sincere.

2. **Trustworthiness.** Employees must keep promises and fulfill commitments.

3. **Loyalty.** Employees must be devoted to their tasks and be true to persons and institutions.

4. **Fairness.** Equal treatment to all employees must prevail.

5. **Caring.** Concern for the well being of others is necessary. Kindness is required.

6. **Respect.** Employees must be courteous and considerate and respect the dignity and privacy of others.

7. **Responsibility.** Employees must be competent to carry out their duties in the best interest of others.

8. **Accountability.** Employees must accept responsibility for their consequences, actions, and decisions in the pursuit of excellence.

ACTIVITIES

1. After an ethical audit by an ad hoc committee of your company, Smith and Brothers, the company was found to be in violation of its ethical code. According to the audit, not all ethical areas were covered by the current code. According to

the audit, the following areas must be covered in any code of ethics:

    a. Safety for products, services, and people
    b. Equal opportunity for employment
    c. Compliance with laws and regulations
    d. Sexual harassment
    e. Personal relationships
    f. Giving of gifts
    g. Private employment outside the company and other conflicting roles
    h. Endorsements

Use the Internet, an annual report, or personal visits to companies to find examples of codes of ethics. Refer to the sample code of ethics on page 164 also. Write a one-page code of ethics for your classroom.

2. Conduct an ethical compliance audit by visiting a company in your area. Ask the following questions and any others you think necessary to find out about the company's code of ethics. Prepare a memo to your instructor giving the results of your research.

    a. Does the company have a code of ethics?
    b. Who is responsible for seeing that the code of ethics is followed?
    c. What happens to people who do not obey the code?
    d. Is the code of ethics made public? Has the code appeared in the newspaper? Is the code made available to all employees of the company?
    e. Is the code listed in the company manual?
    f. How does top management detect the ethical issues that need to be resolved?
    g. How do employees report unethical conduct?
    h. Is the code of ethics under constant scrutiny to see that all areas are covered?
    i. Does your company have an ethics committee?
    j. Is there consistent enforcement of standards and punishments in the organization?
    k. Is the code of ethics updated periodically?

3. Using the Internet and the library, search for information about the Federal Sentencing Guidelines. What do these guidelines have to do with codes of ethics? What influence do these guidelines have on codes of ethics? Write a short memo to

your instructor that summarizes the Federal Sentencing Guidelines and how these guidelines can be used to structure a Code of Ethics for your company.

4. Join in a class discussion with the other class members as to whether or not they have ever worked in a company that has a code of ethics. What were their reactions to working under such a code? Do the workers feel that the code of ethics worked? What were some problems with the code?

5. Have you ever worked at a company that did not have a Code of Ethics? Perhaps the company did have a Code of Ethics and you were not aware of it? How can you find out about the ethical climate at a company in which you work? Discuss.

6. Discuss in a team situation what diversity issues you might need to consider in developing a Code of Ethics? Present your findings orally to the other class members.

RESOURCES

www.ja.org/ethics - defines ethics as rules; illustrations of ethical businesses

www.ethics.org - provides information on ethical practices in business.

http://www.ethicsweb.ca/codes/ - provides instructions on how to write a code of ethics.

CODE OF ETHICS

The Old Frontier Corporation
(Revised January 15, 200x)

The Old Frontier Corporation is committed to treating our employees, our customers, and our suppliers with honesty, integrity, trustworthiness, fairness, respect, reliability, and safety.

1. Honesty and sincerity; truthfulness

2. Unquestionable integrity

3. Ability to keep promises; trustworthiness

4. Respect for all people

5. Reliability; always seeking excellence

6. Safety in the workplace

Guiding Principles

1. The Old Frontier Corporation will obey all laws, rules, and regulations.

2. Products and services will be consistent with quality and safety standards.

3. The Old Frontier Corporation supports and encourages diversity in the workplace. No one will be discriminated against because of race, color, religion, gender, national origin, political affiliation, physical handicap, age, marital status, or sexual orientation.

4. Customer satisfaction with products and services will be a top concern.

5. The Old Frontier Corporation will review and adapt to changing consumer needs and all trends in the marketplace.

The Code of Ethics of The Old Frontier Corporation is designed to establish and maintain a pleasant, safe, and ethical climate in which to work in order to maintain the public's positive image of our company.

TOPIC

Evaluating web site content

KEY POINTS

1. Finding quality information on the Internet requires analysis and critical thinking skills.

2. Written resources found on the Internet must be critically evaluated to determine the quality of the information—all web sites are not created equal.

3. The five most basic criteria to base your evaluation of web sites include:
   a. Accuracy
   b. Authenticity
   c. Objectivity
   d. Currency
   e. Coverage

4. Evaluating the content of web sites involves the analysis of a number of issues related to these five basic criteria, such as:
   a. Is the information dated?
   b. What is the expertise of the author?
   c. Is the information objective?
   d. Is the purpose of the site stated?
   e. Is adequate information provided regarding how
   f. research was conducted, data gathered, etc.?
   g. Are sources cited as to where/how the information was
   h. retrieved?

5. Understanding "who" the author or publisher of a web page is also important. By looking at the address (URL) of the web site you can determine the domain:
   a. Education site – *.edu* in the address
   b. Government site - *.gov* in the address
   c. Commercial site - *.com* in the address
   d. Network site - *.net* in the address

   Be aware that within any given domain there is a wide range of quality. Just because a web site has, for example, an education domain doesn't guarantee the accuracy or quality of the information.

6. Additional resources on evaluating web pages and information on citing web sites can be found on following page.

164

Five Criteria for Evaluating Web Pages

Source: www.library.cornell.edu/okuref/webcrit.html

Evaluation of Web documents

1. *Accuracy of Web Documents*
- Who wrote the page and can you contact him or her?
- What is the purpose of the document and why was it produced?
- Is this person qualified to write this document?

2. *Authority of Web Documents*
- Who published the document, and is it separate from the "Webmaster"?
- Check the domain of the document; what institution publishes this document?
- Does the publisher list his or her qualifications?

3. *Objectivity of Web Documents*
- What goals/objectives does this page meet?
- How detailed is the information?
- What opinions (if any) are expressed by the author?

4. *Currency of Web Documents*
- When was it produced?
- When was it updated?
- How up to date are the links (if any)?

5. *Coverage of the Web Documents*
- Are the links (if any) evaluated and do they complement the documents' themes?
- Is the coverage all images or a balance of text and images?
- Is the information presented cited correctly?

How to interpret the basics

Accuracy
- Make sure author provides email or a contact address/phone number.
- Know the distinction between author and Webmaster.

Authority
- What credentials are listed for the author?
- Where is the document published? Check URL domain.

Objectivity
- Determine if page is a mask for advertising; if so, information might be biased.
- View any web page as you would an infomercial on television; ask why this information was written and for whom?

Currency
- How many dead links are there?
- Are the links current or updated regularly?
- Is the information outdated?

Coverage
- If page requires special software to view, how much are you missing if you don't have the software?
- Is it free or is there a fee for info?
- Is there an option for text only, or frames, or a suggested browser for better viewing?

From *C & RL News,* July/August 1998: 522-523, "Teaching undergrads WEB evaluation: A guide for library instruction" by Jim Kapoun. Copyright © 1998 by Jim Kapoun. Reprinted by permission of the author.

ACTIVITIES

1. Develop your skills for conducting Internet research and evaluating web site content with an *Internet Scavenger Hunt.* Your instructor will provide you with a list of five items for the scavenger hunt.

   a. You must find an exact match for each item listed in the *Scavenger Hunt.*

   b. Read the explanation for each item carefully.

   c. You must provide a hard copy print out of the relevant page.

   d. You must provide the exact address (URL) of the source and know who sponsored that source.

   e. You must find all five items to complete the *Scavenger Hunt.*

   f. You must turn your sources/printouts into the instructor in person (instructor will record time and date).

   g. First person to find all of the items wins!

2. Complete the Internet tutorials on this web site as assigned by your instructor: http://library.albany.edu/internet/

RESOURCES

1. Evaluating Online Resources Notebook
   www.uis.edu/~schroede/valid.htm

2. The Good, the Bad, & the Ugly
   http://lib.nmsu.edu/instruction/eval.html

3. Evaluating Web Sites: Criteria and Tools
   www.library.cornell.edu/okuref/research/webeval.html

4. Evaluating Internet Resources (includes Internet tutorials)
   http://library.albany.edu/internet/evaluate.html

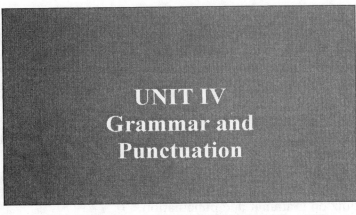

UNIT IV
Grammar and Punctuation

**CAPSTONE PROJECT FOR GRAMMAR AND
PUNCTUATION UNIT IV**

The Capstone Project for Unit IV is designed to develop your writing skills by improving your knowledge of the basic rules of grammar and punctuation and demonstrating your mastery of these rules by successfully completing the *Diagnostic Test on Punctuation, Number Writing, and Capitalization* and the test on *Similar and Confusing Words*.

Complete the *Diagnostic Test on Punctuation, Number Writing, and Capitalization* on pages 169-170. When completed, score your test using the answer key provided on pages 192-193. Review the questions you missed to determine what concepts you need to study. Refer to the appropriate section in this unit to learn more about these concepts and to prepare you to successfully complete the *Diagnostic Test* again at the end of the semester.

1. Take the diagnostic test that appears on pages 169-170 (your instructor may choose to give you a copy of the test or have you place your answers on a separate page).
2. Check your answers to the diagnostic test with the correct answers provided on pages 192-193.
3. Note carefully the questions and concepts you have missed. In the material that follows the test, study carefully the reasons for each rule of punctuation, number usage, and capitalization.
4. Report your score to your instructor, and be sure to keep your test.
5. Study the material in Unit IV.
6. Take the test again at the end of the semester to see if you have improved your results.
7. *Note for optional assignment:* A second punctuation practice test (with answers) is included in the *Appendix* section of this text also.
8. Study the section on *Similar and Confusing Words* on pages 186 through 191. Then take the test on page 194. Check the answers on page 195.
9. Prepare 40 sentences using the material in *Similar and Confusing Words* section. Include your sentences as part of the capstone project for this unit.

http://owl.english.purdue.edu/handouts/grammar/ - an online writing lab (OWL) provided by Purdue University; includes resources and exercises for grammar, punctuation, and spelling.

http://www.grammarbook.com/default.htm - includes grammar and punctuation tests.

http://filebox.vt.edu/eng/mech/writing/handbook/exercises/quiz2.html - includes quiz on grammar and punctuation.

http://news.bbc.co.uk/l/hi/magazine/3256388.stm - includes punctuation quiz.

http://webster.commnet.edu/grammar/ - an online guide to grammar and writing.

DIAGNOSTIC TEST ON PUNCTUATION, NUMBER WRITING, AND CAPITALIZATION

Instructions: Supply the missing punctuation in the following sentences (pencil recommended). Then check your work with the answers on pages 193 and 194. If a sentence needs no corrections, mark "C" for correct as is.

1. Please ship Mr. Harter the television set the computer monitor and the stereo system immediately.

2. My very good friend Ashley Potts moved to the Upper Peninsula of Michigan.

3. We shall miss all you do for us of course.

4. John Houser is a dedicated competent employee.

5. Consequently we cannot give you a raise at this time.

6. Josiah Priestly said, "The office will be closed this coming Friday

7. Everyone said that he was a well qualified worker.

8. Pele played a terrific soccer game he made the winning goal in the last two seconds.

9. My records will show Ms. Blanton that you did not make a payment last month and we must take immediate action against you.

10. We are pleased that you will be moving to Mount Pleasant and we look forward to having you in our firm.

11. If you hear from him before next week please let me know.

12. May I hear from you as soon as possible

13. She told me that her car was a "lemon

14. Jerrod is an author who is very well known.

15. Did she say, "Are you going diving this weekend

16. Luigi Jones turned 32 years old today.

17. 20 people attended the event yesterday.

18. Please make a xerox copy of the plan for me.

19. Hes one of the most responsible persons I know.

20. She is a well known author of childrens books.

21. I want the couch recovered in this type of material.

22. Please pick up your passenger at 3698 West Belmont Street Cleveland Ohio.

23. We will not begin work until Thursday Friday or Saturday of next week.

24. The babys rattle fell into the playpen.

25. The people were unhappy with the decision for instance most of them wanted a vacation day the Friday after thanksgiving.

26. He wanted one half of last months salary.

27. Andrea Cummings is the president elect of her sorority.

28. Please give me the following items immediately one pen two pencils and three reams of paper.

29. Will you come with me Clara

30. The entire family will vacation in yosemite national park in california next month.

31. Nearly sixty % of the people voted in the last election.

32. Her all time favorite movie is gone with the wind.

33. The human relations division of our company is on the cutting edge of what is happening.

34. I just finished reading the novel coming of age in mount pleasant yesterday.

35. The manager fired Consuella from the company on May 1 2002.

36. Yes I knew that Consuella was fired she was lazy in her work for the company.

37. As you very well know we cannot give your order first priority many other orders came in ahead of your's.

38. Thank you very much Senor Valdez for all of the work you have done in our behalf.

39. Albert Rumdum who is old enough to know better plunged into the shallow water head first.

40. She yelled no smoking in the building.

PUNCTUATION

COMMA

Commas with Conjunctions. A comma is used to separate two *independent* clauses joined by a conjunction (and, but, or, nor, for, and others). An *independent clause* is a group of words that has a subject and a verb and that can stand independently as a sentence.

1. Your latest letter came yesterday, and we were glad to hear from you.

2. Almost everyone got to the business meeting on time, but Adrian Collins came a half hour late.

3. The report is due one week from today, or heads will roll.

Comma for Words in a Series. A series is a group of three or more words or items and should be separated by commas.

1. Please send me the following today: the report on new business hours, the report on medical benefits, and the report on employee time schedules.

2. Josiah likes to eat apples, oranges, and bananas.

3. The new employees will arrive on Monday, Tuesday, and Wednesday of next week.

Comma for Apposition. In order to make the meaning of a sentence perfectly clear, the writer may choose to describe something in greater detail. The description is set off with commas.

1. My favorite ex-student is Mari Collingwood, my wife's second cousin.

2. Alfred, the leader of the orchestra, received his training at Jones School of Music.

3. Send the latest report to Stephen Ramsey, the director of the program.

<u>Comma for Direct Address.</u> When talking directly to someone, set off the person's name with a comma or commas.

1. Thanks so much, Mr. Milarski, for the terrific job you did on the report.

2. Mr. Milarski, thanks so much for the terrific job you did on the report.

3. Little girl, are you the one throwing mud at me?

<u>Comma in Parenthetical Expressions.</u> Sometimes a writer will insert a comment or an explanation into a sentence to make the meaning perfectly clear. This inserted material can, if necessary, be omitted from the sentence without changing the meaning of the sentence. These words are called *parenthetical.*

1. Please let me know, however, what the status of your employment is.

2. Of course, you may drop into my office at any time you wish.

3. Moreover, I thought the movie was dull and boring.

<u>Comma with Dates and Expressions.</u> Use a comma after parts of a date and parts of an address.

1. Rogene was fired from the company on June 1, 2002, at 8 a.m.

2. Keith lives at 3987 Westwood, Los Angeles, California.

3. The company will move to 987 North Punxsutawney Avenue, Greenville, Pennsylvania.

<u>Comma for Introductory Expressions.</u> Use commas after introductory words. Some of these words are *if, as, since, when, unless, frankly, otherwise, for instance, for example, moreover, yes, no, well,* and *oh.*

1. Yes, I'll be there just as soon as I can.

2. If you plan to attend the meeting in Dallas, I'll go with you.

3. Since you have been working here, business is humming.

Comma for Nonrestrictive and Restrictive Clauses and Phrases. A *nonrestrictive* clause or phrase is one that may be omitted from the sentence without changing the meaning of the sentence. A *restrictive* clause or phrase is one that may *not* be omitted from the sentence; therefore, no commas are used.

1. Roger Smithson, who is old enough to know better, jumped out the third story of his office building when the elevator wasn't working.

2. Chapters of books that are too technical should be read carefully.

3. The students who get the highest grades in high school will have no trouble entering college.

Comma for Adjectives that Modify. When two or more adjectives modify (describe) the same noun, separate the adjectives with a comma.

1. Georgia is a careful, conscientious person.

2. Most of us like challenging, exciting football games.

3. Scott Macfarlane's new Armani suit is a deep, dark blue color.

Comma to Introduce a Short Quotation. Short quotations are introduced by a comma. (Note: Periods and commas are **always** placed **inside** the final quotation mark.)

1. The officer shouted, "Stop, or I'll shoot."

2. The official sign on the wall stated, "No smoking in this building."

3. "I must," Natalie said, "get this office cleaned before the boss gets back."

PERIOD

Periods with Declarative and Imperative Sentences. Use a period after a declarative sentence (one that states a fact) or an imperative sentence (one that states a command).

1. Stop that noise immediately.

2. I love Paris in the spring.

3. Shirley's all-time favorite movie is *Gone with the Wind.*

Periods with Courteous Requests. After a request for definite action, a period, rather than a question mark, is used.

1. May we hear from you after you have read the report.

2. Will you please let us know what you think about the report.

3. Will you type this report immediately.

Periods with Abbreviations. Use a period with abbreviations.

1. Send the package f.o.b. to Natasha Freeloader, Ph.D.

2. Mr. Collins and Mrs. Lewis will co-chair the annual charity ball.

3. Be sure to call me at 8:00 a.m.—not 7:00 a.m.

SEMICOLON

Semicolon—No Conjunction. A semicolon is used to separate two independent, but closely related clauses (sentences that can stand alone) when a conjunction is *not* used.

1. Audrey will become the new president; Mary will be promoted to the vice presidency.

2. Please be at the meeting on time; the meeting will be a short one.

3. I love Paris in the spring; I love Mount Pleasant in the summer.

Semicolon Because a Comma is Present. A comma is used to separate two independent clauses that are joined by a conjunction. However, a comma sometimes occurs within one or both of the independent clauses. When this situation occurs, a *semicolon* is used between the independent clauses that are joined by a conjunction.

1. Otherwise, Amy Macfarlane cannot be at the meeting tomorrow; but I hope to see her at next month's meeting.

2. Brunhilda, however, jumped on her broom; and she flew off into the sunset.

3. Reginald Properman, my neighbor in Mount Pleasant, is decorating his yard with lots of plants; but his wife is not sure she likes what he is doing.

Semicolon Used for Illustrations. When an illustration is introduced by an expression, such as *for example, that is, namely, such as,* a semicolon followed by a comma should precede the expression.

1. Buffy has a clear-cut ambition; that is, to be the greatest vampire slayer the world has ever known.

2. Buffy has another clear-cut ambition; namely, to be able to fly without using an airplane.

3. The members were not happy with the decision; for instance, why would anyone want to hold more meetings?

APOSTROPHE

Apostrophe—Singular Possession. Use an apostrophe then an *s* to show singular possession.

1. The baby's diaper fell off unexpectedly.

2. Goldie's presentation was too long.

3. Our factory's new manager, Hillary Roddy, was fired yesterday.

Apostrophe—Plural Possession. A plural noun ending in *s* calls for an apostrophe *after* the *s* to form the possessive. An irregular plural calls for an apostrophe *before* the *s* to form the possessive.

1.   Someone stole all the girls' soccer balls.

2.   The children's graduation from kindergarten was set for 2:30 p.m.

3.   Not all of the boys' ideas were acceptable.

Apostrophe—Possessive Form of Pronouns. The possessive forms of pronouns do *not* require an apostrophe.

1.   His books were scattered all over the place.

2.   Her dedication to the job is questionable.

3.   The dog lost its collar and its leash.

Apostrophe—Replacing Letters. Use an apostrophe to replace letters omitted in a contraction.

1.   She's the finest person I know.

2.   It's not too late to start drilling for oil.

3.   Doesn't she want to marry him?

HYPHEN

Hyphens—Compound Expressions. Hyphens are used in compound expressions when a *noun* follows the expression. When a noun *does not* follow the compound expression, no hyphen is used.

1.   Steve and Wendy Williams are well-known authors of scary, occult books.

2.   Steven Egler is a world-class organist.

3.   Rufus wants to work full time, but his boss will only pay him for part-time work.

Hyphens—for Word Division. Use a hyphen to divide words between syllables at the end of a line.

1. The meeting will con-   vene at 2:00 p.m.

2. We moved all of the cor-   porate offices to the ninth floor.

3. He stops everyone in the hall for a short   con-versation.

Hyphens in Compound Numbers. Use a hyphen with compound numbers and with fractions.

1. Mary Lucas, my top-notch secretary, turned thirty-one today.

2. Please give me one-half of your pizza.

3. One-fourth of the world's population lives in poverty.

Hyphens for Clarity of a Word. Use a hyphen in a word that needs to be clarified.

1. Did you re-cover that chair that was recovered after the theft?

2. Wendy remarked, "He re-marked the merchandise."

3. The reformed convict re-formed his escape plan.

Hyphens in Compound Titles. Use a hyphen with compound titles.

1. Greg Beamer is president-elect of his fraternity.

2. The ex-president of the fraternity is Colin Douglas.

3. Both Colin and Greg are ex-students of mine.

COLON

Colon with a Listing. Use a colon to show that something is to follow. The material that appears *before* the colon must be a complete independent thought. When the material following the colon is a complete sentence, begin the sentence with a capital letter.

1. Please bring me carrots, potatoes, and celery for the stew. (No colon)

2. Please bring me the following for the stew: carrots, potatoes, and celery.

3. Bring a notepad, pencils, pens, and paper clips to the office today.

Colon for Other Uses. Use a colon after a salutation in a business letter and when using numbers to indicate time, volume, or page.

1. Dear Mr. Robinson:

2. Scott and Amy will be here at 8:30 a.m., not 8:30 p.m.

3. The citation is from Richard's article, 8:15 (meaning volume 8, page 15).

QUESTION MARK

Question Mark with a Question. Use a question mark at the end of a question.

1. Will you go with me?

2. What time will the ball game start?

3. Do you have any idea about the report I'm supposed to complete?

Question Mark Inside the Quotation Marks. If the quoted part of a sentence is a question, place the question mark *inside* the final quotation mark.

1. James replied, "Did she really say that?"

2. Julie asked, "Will you be at the family reunion next year?"

3. "Have you slain any vampires lately?" Buffy asked.

Question Mark Outside the Quotation Marks. If the entire sentence is a question and contains quoted matter, the question mark is placed *outside* the quotation mark.

1. Did Buffy ask, "What's to become of me"?

2. Did Ralph say, "What happened to the rest of my sandwich"?

3. Who said, "I have but one life to give for my country"?

DASH AND PARENTHESIS

Dashes and Parentheses. Use a dash to indicate an abrupt change of thought or to indicate a parenthetical expression. Use parentheses to indicate numbered sections with sentences and to enclose words that explain. The dash is a stronger mark of punctuation than are parentheses.

1. Please buy me (1) a carrot, (2) a stick of celery, (3) two potatoes, and (4) three beets for my soup.

2. Uncle George (my least favorite person) moved to Georgia.

3. Please know—whether you understand or not—that I am in charge of this operation.

EXCLAMATION POINT

Exclamation Point. Use an exclamation point after a word or a phrase and at the end of a sentence to express surprise or a strong emotion.

1. I hate this boring lecture!

2. Don't hurt yourself by falling into the rapids!

3. Awesome!

NUMBER USAGE

Numbers at Beginning of Sentence. When a number is the first word of a sentence, spell the number in full.

      1.   Eighty people attend the barbecue.

      2.   Thirty-three years ago we moved to Michigan.

      3.   Nineteen hundred fifty-three was a very good year.

Numbers Appearing Together. When two numbers appear in succession, spell out the smaller number and place the larger number in figures.

      1.   Send me two 8-gallon cans of ice cream.

      2.   At the party, three 70-year olds were honored.

      3.   Seven 60-year old men attended the reunion.

Numbers 11 and Over. One basic rule of using numbers is to use figures to express most numbers 11 and over. Generally spell out a number ten and under. Spell out a number at the beginning of a sentence. **(Note: Many exceptions occur to this rule. Be certain you are aware of these exceptions.)**

      1.   Over 15 people attended the barbecue.

      2.   Fewer that ten students were absent the entire year.

      3.   One hundred teachers were at the last meeting of the union; the union has over 300 members.

Numbers with Age. Use numbers to express someone's *exact* age; use words to express *general references* to age.

      1.   Marilu is 34 years old today. Her husband, John, is approximately thirty-one years of age.

      2.   Shirley Gersna is exactly 50 years old today.

      3.   Jose will be 19 tomorrow.

Numbers for Small Fractions and Periods of Time. Use words to express small fractions and periods of time.

1.   One-half of the money is mine.

2.   I saw her about ten days ago.

3.   Can you at least be prompt three-fourths of the time?

Numbers to Express Time. Use figures to express time and dates. Place the time in *figures* when using a.m. or p.m. (A.M. or P.M.). However, place the time in *words* when using o'clock.

1.   Please meet me under the clock at the department store by 2:30 p.m.

2.   I'll see you on June 13, 200x, at eight o'clock at the restaurant.

3.   Please be at the 3:30 p.m. meeting on April 10, 200x.

Numbers for Money and Percentages. Use figures for expressing dollars, cents, and percent. Use a combination of figures and words to express sums of one million dollars and over.

1.   Over 15 percent of the employees were eligible for the bonus of $350 for their work. (Omit the decimal and zeros for even sums of money.)

2.   That lollipop costs 37 cents.

3.   The stock dropped 14 percent in one-half hour causing us to take a $4 million loss.

Numbers for Addresses. Use numbers when expressing house numbers, apartment numbers, and street numbers over ten.

1.   Maribel lives at 264 West 16 Street.

2.   Martha lives at 9877 West Tenth Street (spell out number 10 or under).

3.   Our office is at 3968 North 100 Street, Room 16.

Numbers for Weights, Distances, and Measures. Use numbers when expressing weights, distances, and measurements, even if those numbers are ten or under.

1.   Louise drove 8 miles to visit her boyfriend.

2.   Sam's weight went from 300 to 385 pounds.

3.   The box is 3 feet by 4 feet.

Numbers with Days and Years. Use numbers for days of the month and for years.

1.   I saw her April 12, 200x, at the stock exchange.

2.   She is a product of the wild 1960s.

3.   I enjoyed the 1990s immensely.

Numbers as Identifiers. When a number is used for identification, place the number in figures.

1.   Please switch the television to channel 12.

2.   Driving down Interstate 96, I passed the university.

3.   John's son is known as John IV.

Numbers in Legal or Commercial Writing. Repeat the number in words or figures in legal and commercial documents.

1.   The attorney's bill came to three thousand ($3,000) dollars.

2.   The bill of lading costs were over one hundred fifty-nine ($159) dollars.

3.   When I had my will prepared, the cost came to over two hundred ($200) dollars.

CAPITALIZATION

Capitalize Proper Nouns. Capitalize the *specific* names of persons, places, and things.

1. John Lucasta was with us when we visited Yellowstone National Park in Wyoming.

2. Please make a duplicate copy of the recipe for French bread.

3. Amy attended Central Michigan University and received a Master of Business Administration degree.

Common Nouns. Common nouns are those that make *general* reference instead of *specific* reference. Do *not* capitalize common nouns.

1. Alyssa Williams received a master's degree in business administration last spring. (Names of seasons are not capitalized.)

2. Nicholas Henegar attended a community college and studied foreign languages and business.

3. Holly Macfarlane was a sales representative for Jackson and Jonas, Inc.

First Word of a Sentence. Capitalize the first word of a sentence. Always capitalize the word "I."

1. Maxine survived the hurricane.

2. CEO Lucas Macfarlane wants the report today.

3. The last time I asked for a raise, I didn't get it.

Capitalize Principal Words. Capitalize the principal words in titles of books, magazines, newspapers, articles, movies, plays, songs, reports, poems, and the like.

NOTE: Use *italics* for books, magazines, newspapers, movies and films, television shows, and plays. Use "quotation marks" for short stories, song titles, poems, articles, and chapters.

1.   Have you read the book, *Working for Peanuts? (Italics* for book titles.)

2.   Lauren Henegar wrote the article entitled "I Don't Like Working for Peanuts," (articles in "quotes") to be included as a chapter in *Work, Work, Work*. (*italics for book titles*)

3.   My favorite movie is *Dumb and Dumber*. (*Italics for movie titles.*)

Capitalize Proper Names, the Names of Specific People, Places, and Organizations.
Use capital letters for proper names, names of specific people, and organizations.

1.   Lucas Macfarlane, Tyler Williams, Jacob Williams, and Mari Featheringham all work for the Perry Corporation in Big Rapids, Michigan.

2.   The Supreme Court of the United States is the final legal authority.

3.   Yellowstone National Park is administered by the United States Government.

Capitalize the Names of National, Political, Racial, Social, Civic, and Athletic Groups. Use capital letters for names of national, political, racial, social, civic, and athletic groups.

1.   The Cleveland Browns are my favorite National Football League Team.

2.   The Democrats, not the Republicans, want to revisit the bill.

3.   Americans for Freedom from Drudgery are hosting a Festival of Life.

Capitalize Trademarks, Events, and Periods. Use capital letters for trademarks, events, and periods.

1. The Great Depression was a disaster.

2. Coca-Cola is a registered United States trademark.

3. One of the most popular software packages is Microsoft Word.

Capitalize Religious Figures, Holy Books, and Holidays. Use capital letters for names of religious figures, holy books, and holidays.

1. My favorite holiday is Thanksgiving; my wife's favorite holiday is Mother's Day.

2. Did you know that God gave the Ten Commandments to Moses?

3. The Holy Bible is the book of the Christian religion.

Capitalize Committee, Department, and Divisions within *Your* Organization.
Outside your organization, capitalize only *specific committee, department, and divisions.*

1. The Marketing Research Department of our company takes care of all of the advertising.

2. You should send the report to their marketing department.

3. Our Personnel Division is a unique organization.

SIMILAR AND CONFUSING WORDS

Some common words sound alike or may even be spelled similarly. Be sure to check in the dictionary any word or words that you suspect may not be correct.

Accept/Except

Accept is a verb that means to receive or agree. Mary will accept the award for winning the prize.

Except is a preposition that means all but or other than. All of the employees received a bonus except for Shirley.

Affect/Effect

Affect is a verb that means to influence, change, or alter. Will his cheating affect everyone in the class?

Effect is a noun that means the result or the consequence or to create or a verb that means "to bring about." What are the effects of the changes in the policy?

Aisle/Isle/I'll

An **aisle** is a passageway. The bride came down the aisle on the arm of her father.

An **isle** is an island. He was marooned on an isle in the Pacific.

I'll is a contraction of I will. I'll be there shortly.

All ready/Already

All ready is used as an adjective that means to be prepared. We were all ready to take the plunge into the pool.

Already is an adverb that refers to time. We were already there when she came.

All right/Alright

All right is two words and is used as an adverb or an adjective. Will you be all right without me?

Alright is an alternate spelling of all right. Second choice. Use the first form. John is either all right or all wrong.

All together/Altogether

All together is an adverb that means everything is a whole. All together, there were 50 people present.

Altogether is an adverb that means completely or entirely. Her report puts an altogether different slant on the subject.

Amount/Number

Amount is used for things in bulk. Send me a large amount of the sugar substitute.

Number is used for individual items. We had a large number of people attend the poetry session.

Anxious/Eager

Anxious implies fear, worry, or concern. I am anxious about his entry into medical school.

Eager means desirous. I am eager to attend the basketball game this evening.

Anyone/Any one

Anyone is a pronoun that means any person at all. Is anyone here?

Any one means a specific item in a group. Any one of those boys could serve as president of the group.

Anyway/Any way

Anyway is an adverb that means in any case. She got the divorce anyway.

Any way means any particular course or direction. Any way you want it is the way I want it, too.

Between/Among

Between is used when referring to comparisons of two persons or things either individually or in pairs. Do I have to choose between Mary and Lois as my prom date?

Among is used when referring to more than two persons or things. Do I have to choose among Mary and Lois and Gretchen as my prom date?

Choose/Chose

To choose is to select. Whom do you choose for your side?

Chose is the past tense of choose. I chose Abigail for our team yesterday.

Conscious/Conscience

Conscious is an adjective that means awake or knowing. Even though I was run over by the tractor, I still was conscious.

Conscience is a noun that means the sense of obligation to be good or a regard for fairness. Mary's conscience wouldn't permit her to cheat on the CPA examination.

Fewer/Less

Fewer refers to number and is used with *plural* nouns. Fewer people than we expected attended the class reunion last month.

Less refers to degree or amount and is used with *singular* nouns. Less sympathy was given to the criminal.

I/Me

I is used as a subject. I am going. John and I are going.

Me is used as an object. Vote for me. Give it to Harold and me.

Idol/Idle/Idyll

Idol is a false god. The pagans worshipped idols.

Idle means to be inactive. Mary was dismissed from her job and remained idle for over two months.

Idyll is a simple, pastoral scene. The lambs gathering for their food is a perfect picture of an idyll.

Illegible/Ineligible

Illegible means something is unreadable. Her handwriting was completely illegible.

Ineligible means unqualified. An ineligible receiver was downfield.

Illicit/Elicit

Illicit is something illegal. He was arrested for selling illicit drugs.

Elicit is to draw something out. I will elicit as much information from her as I can.

Immigrant/Emigrant

An immigrant is one who enters a country. Joseph is an immigrant from Australia.

An emigrant is one who leaves a country. Joe emigrated to the United States; that fact makes him an emigrant.

Immoral/Amoral

Immoral is evil. The ruler of the country was an immoral man.

Amoral is without a sense of moral responsibility. He was completely amoral when it came to firing seven employees.

Incite/Insight

Incite means to stir up. Was it Raymond who incited the riot?

Insight is a keen understanding. Ramona has insight of the smallest details.

Insane/Inane

To drive someone insane is to drive him or her mad. Are you insane?

Inane means pointless. His strategy was inane.

Intense/Intents

Intense means an extreme degree. He is completely intense on getting that project done by tomorrow.

Intents are purposes. His intents are to disrupt the meeting and halt progress.

Irrelevant/Irreverent

Irrelevant is not pertinent. Those figures you quoted were completely irrelevant.

Irreverent is disrespectful. His ideas on the whole matter were irreverent.

Its/It's

Its is a possessive pronoun. The dog buried its bone in the back yard.

It's is a contraction for it is. It's my duty to watch out for you until you are an adult.

Its' is not a word in the English language; therefore, no use exists for its'.

Loose/Lose

Loose is not tight. That sweater is too loose on you.

Lose means fail to win. Did you lose the battle yesterday?

Principal/Principle

Principal means man or woman, main, and money. The principal of the school provided the principal idea to pay off the principal and the interest.

Principle is a rule of conduct. She has excellent moral principles.

Stationary/Stationery

Stationary means not moving. Rose rides a stationary bike for exercise.

Stationery means paper. Send the letter on high-quality stationery.

Than/Then

Than is used in comparison statements, in statements of preference, and to suggest quantities beyond a specified amount. She is prettier than I. I would rather eat beans than peas. I want you to study more than just the basics.

Then is a time other than the present time or next in time, space or order. Then I told him to quit fighting. Do this job first, and then we can move on to the next one.

Who/Whom

Who **is subjective**. Who is going to pay this bill?

Whom **is objective, used after a preposition**. She is the one to whom I spoke.

We're, Where, Were

We're **is a contraction for we are**. We're glad to be here.

Where **is a place or a location**. Where are you going tomorrow?

Were **is the past tense of the verb** *be*. They were heading out to the restaurant.

Your/You're

Your **is a possessive pronoun**. Your place in line is secure.

You're **is a contraction of you and are**. You're my favorite person here..

Their/There/They're

Their **is a possessive pronoun**. All the students have their books.

There **is a place**. There is my book; her book is over there.

They're **is a contraction of they are**. They're going to be there with their books before noon.

To/Too/Two

To **is a preposition that indicates direction**. We all went to the Happy Hour after work yesterday.

Too **means very or also**. John was too excited to even speak. Mary was excited, too.

Two **is the number 2**. Two of us attended the party. The two of us went to school, too.

ANSWERS TO DIAGNOSTIC TEST ON PUNCTUATION, NUMBER WRITING, AND CAPITALIZATION

Instructions: **Check your answers for the diagnostic test on pages 169 and 170 with the ones that follow. Study the items you have missed by reviewing that topic in Unit IV.**

1. Please ship Mr. Harter the television set, the computer monitor, and the stereo system immediately.

2. My very good friend, Ashley Potts, moved to the Upper Peninsula of Michigan.

3. We shall miss all you do for us, of course.

4. John Houser is a dedicated, competent employee.

5. Consequently, we cannot give you a raise at this time.

6. Josiah Priestly said, "The office will be closed this coming Friday."

7. Everyone said that he was a well-qualified worker.

8. Pele played a terrific soccer game; he made the winning goal in the last two seconds.

9. My records will show, Ms. Blanton, that you did not make a payment last month; and we must take immediate action against you.

10. We are pleased that you will be moving to Mount Pleasant, and we look forward to having you in our firm.

11. If you hear from him before next week, please let me know.

12. May I hear from you as soon as possible.

13. She told me that her car was a "lemon."

14. Jerrod is an author who is very well known.

15. Did she say, "Are you going diving this weekend"?

16. Luigi Jones turned 32 years old today.

17. Twenty people attended the event yesterday.

18. Please make a Xerox copy of the plan for me.

19. He's one of the most responsible persons I know.

20. She is a well-known author of children's books.

21. I want the couch re-covered in this type of material.

22. Please pick up your passenger at 3698 West Belmont Street, Cleveland, Ohio.

23. We will not begin work until Thursday, Friday, or Saturday of next week.

24. The baby's rattle fell into the playpen.

25. The people were unhappy with the decision; for instance, most of them wanted a vacation day the Friday after Thanksgiving.

26. He wanted one-half of last month's salary.

27. Andrea Cummings is the president-elect of her sorority.

28. Please give me the following items immediately: one pen, two pencils, and three reams of paper.

29. "Will you come with me, Clara"?

30. The entire family will vacation in Yosemite National Park in California next month.

31. Nearly 60 percent of the people voted in the last election.

32. Her all-time favorite movie is "Gone with the Wind."

33. The Human Relations Division of our company is on the cutting edge of what is happening.

34. I just finished reading the novel, "Coming of Age in Mount Pleasant," yesterday.

35. The manager fired Consuella from the company on May 1, 2002.

36. Yes, I knew that Consuella was fired; she was lazy in her work for the company.

37. As you very well know, we cannot give your order first priority; many other orders came in ahead of yours.

38. Thank you very much, Senor Valdez, for all of the work you have done in our behalf.

39. Albert Rumdum, who is old enough to know better, plunged into the shallow water head first.

40. She yelled, "No smoking in the building."

DIAGNOSTIC TEST
SIMILAR AND CONFUSING WORDS

Instructions: Circle the word or words to complete the sentence correctly (answers are on the next page).

1. We walked the (aisle, isle, I'll) holding on to the usher.

2. All of the candidates addressed the audience (accept, except) me.

3. Many people worship movie stars as (idols, idles, Idylls).

4. She is (illegible, ineligible) for the position.

5. (It's, Its) my party.

6. Please do not (loose, lose) the car keys again.

7. John will serve as (principal, principle) of the high school this year.

8. She bought him a (stationary, stationery) bicycle for his exercises.

9. All contestants took (their, there, they're) place at the starting line.

10. Do you think his sickness will (affect, effect) his school work?

11. We were (all ready, already) (their, there, they're) when the bell rang.

12. Was (anyone, any one) at home when you called?

13. John said he was (all right, alright) after the accident.

14. Vote for John Johnson and (I, me).

15. Marijuana is an (illicit, elicit) drug.

16. (Who, Whom) will pay the bill?

17. (Your, You're) such a nice person.

18. The (to, too, two) of us attended that school, (to, too, two).

19. He has (fewer, less) brains than the rest of us, I think.

20. Even though he fell and hit his head, he was still (conscious, conscience).

21. Who (incited, insighted) the riot?

22. Read this book (than, then) you can read the second one.

23. A large (amount, number) of food fed a large (amount, number) of people.

24. Joe read (fewer, less) books (than, then) Bill; however, (fewer, less) time existed.

195

ANSWERS TO DIAGNOSTIC TEST
SIMILAR AND CONFUSING WORDS

1. We walked the *aisle* holding on to the usher.

2. All of the candidates addressed the audience *except* me.

3. Many people worship movie stars as *idols*.

4. She is *ineligible* for the position.

5. *It's* my party.

6. Please do not *lose* the car keys again.

7. John will serve as *principal* of the high school this year.

8. She bought him a *stationary* bicycle for his exercises.

9. All contestants took *their* place at the starting line.

10. Do you think his sickness will *affect* his school work?

11. We were *already there* when the bell rang.

12. Was *anyone* at home when you called?

13. John said he was *all right* after the accident.

14. Vote for John Johnson and *me*.

15. Marijuana is an *illicit* drug.

16. *Who* will pay the bill?

17. *You're* such a nice person.

18. The *two* of us attended that school, *too*.

19. He has *fewer* brains than the rest of us, I think.

20. Even though he fell and hit his head, he was still *conscious*.

21. Who *incited* the riot?

22. Read this book *then* you can read the second one.

23. A large *amount* of food fed a large *number* of people.

24. Joe read *fewer* books *than* Bill; however, *less* time existed.

APPENDIX

Teaching Tools and Forms

Evaluation Form for
Employment Communication Unit I Capstone Project (150 pts.)

Name _____

Cover Letter - 20 pts. total
____ Block format, date, proper punctuation in salutation, closing, includes "enclosure." <u>5 pts.</u>
____ Proper punctuation, grammar, sentence structure, proper spelling. <u>6 pts.</u>
____ References company name and specific person/or title directed to
    -first sentence states purpose/position applying for; first paragraph includes a positive
    reference (compliment) to the company. <u>5 pts.</u>
____ Addresses and references specific qualifications of the position, e.g. refers to
relevant education and/or work experience; refers to "enclosed resume" and includes "call
to action", e.g. requests interview. <u>4 pts.</u>

Unsolicited Cover Letter – 20 pts. total
____ Block format, date, proper punctuation in salutation, closing, includes "enclosure." <u>5 pts.</u>
____ Proper punctuation, grammar, sentence structure, proper spelling. <u>6 pts.</u>
____ References company name and specific person/or title directed to and refers to "enclosed
resume." <u>5 pts.</u>
____ Addresses and references potential qualifications of the position, e.g. refers to
relevant education and/or work experience; refers to "enclosed resume" and references
future possibility for employment. <u>4 pts.</u>

Resume – 50 pts.
____ Appealing overall format; appropriate white space, variation in font sizes used, variety of
special effects used, includes header on any additional pages. <u>10 pts.</u>

____ Proper punctuation, grammar, spelling, and consistent format throughout. <u>10 pts.</u>

____ Guidelines followed, e.g. no abbreviations, name is largest font size used, dates are
consistent format, easy to find and follow; sections of resume are in proper
sequence (education first, then work experience). <u>10 pts.</u>

____ Relevant and required information is included: <u>15 pts.</u>
- Education includes degree, major, city, state, expected date of graduation;
- Work experience includes month and year, company name, city, state, job title, job
  duties (as applicable with consistent, parallel descriptions using past tense for previous
  work experience), job duty descriptions are appropriate and effectively phrased;
- Other activities, memberships, and/or special skills sections included as appropriate
  with complete information, accurate descriptions, and necessary dates.

____ Irrelevant or unnecessary information is not included - personal information,
outdated information, inappropriate information. <u>5 pts.</u>

Scannable Resume – 20 pts.

_____ Use of sans serif font like Arial or Optima (not Times New Roman). 3 pts.

_____ Proper punctuation, grammar, spelling, etc. 5 pts.

_____ Use same font and font size (appropriate) on the entire document. 4 pts.

_____ Appropriate use of formatting; letter / characters do not touch; no ampersands, percent signs, all caps, bullets, graphics, boxes, or columns. 5 pts.

_____ Left-justify every line; appropriate spacing. 3 pts.

Follow-up Thank You Letter – 20 pts.

_____ Block format, date, proper punctuation in salutation and closing. 7 pts.

_____ Proper punctuation, grammar, sentence structure, spelling. 7 pts.

_____ References specific job title and specific person directed to. 6 pts.

    -first sentence states purpose of letter and refers to position specifically.

Common Interview Question w/answers – 10 pts.

_____Answers outlined and well thought out. 5 pts.

_____Answers all questions from list as assigned. 5 pts.

Printouts Internet resources – 10 pts.

_____Resumes resources. 5 pts.

_____Interview resources. 5 pts.

_____ **TOTAL POINTS** (150 pts. possible)

Name _____

ORAL REPORT to Inform
Evaluation Form

Component

Organization	Yes	No
❑ Effective opening – introduces topic/purpose.		
❑ Initiates rapport with audience.		
❑ Time limit is observed.		
❑ Effective ending is utilized; concisely summarized.		

Delivery	Yes	No
❑ Appropriate eye contact is used.		
❑ "Nonword" and other annoying speech habits are avoided.		
❑ Distracting body language (leaning, tapping, etc.) is avoided.		
❑ Gestures and body language are used appropriately.		
❑ A relaxed, confident appearance is exhibited.		
❑ Effectively articulates words.		
❑ Rate of speech is appropriate; pauses effectively.		

Content	Yes	No
❑ Information is accurate and current.		
❑ A few major points are included; adequate support for each.		
❑ Attention-getter is used and effective.		
❑ Visual aid is used; is well designed; discussed appropriately.		

Comments (discuss at least 1 strength and 1 weakness of this speaker):

Directions: Put your name in the space provided and give the form to members of your audience.

Name _____

ORAL REPORT to INFORM
Peer Evaluation Form

Component

Organization	√ Good	Avg.	Fair
❑ Effective opening – introduces topic/purpose.			
❑ Introduces main points, then discusses each.			
❑ Time limit is observed (2-3 minutes).			
❑ Effective ending is utilized; summarizes main points.			

Delivery	√ Good	Avg.	Fair
❑ Appropriate eye contact is used.			
❑ "Nonwords" (um, ah, etc.) are avoided.			
❑ Distracting body language (leaning, tapping, etc.) is avoided.			
❑ Gestures and body language are used appropriately.			
❑ A relaxed, confident appearance is exhibited.			
❑ Effectively articulates words; appropriate rate of speech.			

Content	√ Good	Avg.	Fair
❑ Succeeds at communicating topic.			
❑ A few major points are included; adequate support for each.			
❑ Visual aid is used effectively.			

Comments (list one strength and one weakness of this speaker):

TEAM PRESENTATION EVALUATION FORM

Topic _____ Date _____

Team Members _____

_____

Organization
☐ Effective opening – introduces topic/purpose.   1 2 3 4 5 6 7 8 9 10
☐ Initiates rapport with audience.   1 2 3 4 5 6 7 8 9 10
☐ Time limit is observed; each team member participated. 1 2 3 4 5 6 7 8 9 10
☐ Effective ending is utilized; concisely summarized.   1 2 3 4 5 6 7 8 9 10

Comments _____
_____
_____

Delivery
☐ Appropriate eye contact is used.   1 2 3 4 5 6 7 8 9 10
☐ Nonword and other annoying speech habits are avoided.   1 2 3 4 5 6 7 8 9 10
☐ Distracting body language is avoided.   1 2 3 4 5 6 7 8 9 10
☐ Gestures and body language are used appropriately.   1 2 3 4 5 6 7 8 9 10
☐ A relaxed, confident appearance is exhibited.   1 2 3 4 5 6 7 8 9 10
☐ Effectively articulates words   1 2 3 4 5 6 7 8 9 10
☐ Rate and volume of speech is appropriate.   1 2 3 4 5 6 7 8 9 10

Comments _____
_____
_____

Content
☐ Information is accurate and relevant.   1 2 3 4 5 6 7 8 9 10
☐ Outline of presentation includes key elements (intro.,
  body, summary/concl., attn. getter, humor, v. aids)   1 2 3 4 5 6 7 8 9 10
☐ An appropriate number of major points are included;
  adequate support for each.   1 2 3 4 5 6 7 8 9 10
☐ Training materials provided to audience are effective.   1 2 3 4 5 6 7 8 9 10
☐ Attention-getter is used and effective.   1 2 3 4 5 6 7 8 9 10
☐ Visual aids are used by each team member;
  are well designed; discussed appropriately.   1 2 3 4 5 6 7 8 9 10

Comments _____
_____
_____

OVERALL EVALUATION   1 2 3 4 5 6 7 8 9 10

Team Presentation Evaluation Form **85 pts.**

Component/Criteria

Organization	5 4 3 2 1
❑ Effective opening – introduces topic/purpose.	
❑ Establishes rapport with audience.	
❑ Time limit is observed.	
❑ Effective ending is utilized; concisely summarized.	

Delivery	5 4 3 2 1
❑ Appropriate eye contact is used.	
❑ "Nonword" and other annoying speech habits are avoided.	
❑ Distracting body language (leaning, tapping, etc.) is avoided.	
❑ Gestures and body language are used appropriately.	
❑ A relaxed, confident appearance is exhibited.	
❑ Effectively articulates words.	
❑ Rate of speech is appropriate; pauses effectively.	

Content (*includes hard copy requirements)	5 4 3 2 1
❑ Information is accurate and clearly presented (incl. outline/PP slides)	
❑ Graphs/visual aids are accurate; adequate support for each.	
❑ Visual aids are well designed/effective; each team member uses.	
❑ Findings are provided with adequate explanation/supported by data.	
❑ Outline of presentation uses proper form/complete	
❑ Printout of PP slides turned in (includes copy of survey)	
Comments:	

TEAM MEMBER PEER EVALUATION FORM

List the names of *all* team members, including yourself, in the spaces provided below. Rate yourself and your team members on the relative contribution made to preparing and presenting the material for this assignment. *Your ratings will be confidential and anonymous.* Be honest on this evaluation.

In rating yourself and your team members, use a one to five point scale as follows: *5 = superior, 4 = above average, 3 = average, 2 = below average, and 1 = weak.*

Add the scores to obtain a total score for yourself and the other team members. Put any comments in the space provided at the bottom of this form. Fold this sheet when you complete the ratings to be turned in to your professor.

Include your name <u>and</u> each team member's name in the spaces provided on the next line.						
Names:						
Ratings (see scale above)						
On time for all team meetings						
Helped keep group cohesive						
Contributed useful ideas						
Contributed equal share of work (quality and quantity)						
Total Scores:						

Audience Evaluation Form

Directions: Circle the number you feel best answers each question according to the following scale:

5 = Very Good   4 = Good   3 = Somewhat   2 = A Little   1 = Not at all

_____

1. To what extent did the content of this team's
    training session prepare you to conduct
    business in this country?   5   4   3   2   1

    Comments: _____

    _____

2. To what extent were the visual aids and training materials
    used, appropriate for the presentation of the topic?

                                                                 5   4   3   2   1

    Comments: _____

    _____

3. To what extent did the team present the topic in
    an organized and understandable manner?   5   4   3   2   1

    Comments: _____

    _____

4. To what extent did the team make the material
    interesting?   5   4   3   2   1

    Comments: _____

    _____

5. To what extent do you feel your knowledge and
    understanding of conducting business in this country
    increase as a result of this presentation?   5   4   3   2   1

    Comments: _____

    _____

PowerPoint SLIDE PRESENTATION RUBRIC — 70 pts.			
Template	Template used sets tone and establishes focus of presentation. 9-10 pts.	Template used distracts viewer from presentation. 5-8 pts.	No template used; blank background. 0-4 pts.
Content	Text provides concise information; uses phrases of parallel structure; length of text is appropriate; avoids abbreviations and acronyms. 9-10 pts.	Text provides information with parallel structure; is wordy and too lengthy per slide; uses some abbreviations and acronyms. 5-8 pts.	Text does not provide useful information; is not of parallel structure; is wordy and too lengthy per slide; uses abbreviations and acronyms. 0-4 pts.
Special Effects	Special effects are used to add to the presentation 9-10 pts.	Special effects detract from the presentation 5-8 pts.	No special effects are used 0-4 pts.
Colors	Colors chosen are appealing to the eye and easy to read 9-10 pts.	Some colors chosen are difficult to read 5-8 pts.	Colors chosen distract from the presentation 0-4 pts.
Graphics	Graphics selected always support data or information appropriately; appropriate number of graphics is always selected. 9-10 pts.	Graphics selected could have been better at time(s); too many graphics or not enough graphics are used on some slides. 5-8 pts.	Graphics selected do not represent data or info appropriately; too many graphics or not enough graphics are used on most slides. 0-4 pts..
Spelling	All words are spelled correctly 9-10 pts.	Minor spelling errors 5-8 pts.	Major spelling errors—would be unacceptable in a business setting 0-4 pts.
Grammar	Free of grammatical errors 9-10 pts.	Minor grammatical errors 5-8 pts.	Major grammatical errors—would be unacceptable in a business setting 0-4 pts.

Student Mini Feedback (use at the end of a class or lecture on a topic, etc.)

1. (a) Write down the best thing you learned today.

    (b) Write down one way you will be able to use this new
        "knowledge" in your life.

2. Write down anything you feel confused about from today's class.

Guest Speaker Presentation MEMO Assignment

Directions: Use the memo below to briefly summarize what the guest speaker discussed. Include two (2) things discussed by the speaker that you feel are most relevant to you and why.

TO: **Professor ....**

FROM:

DATE:

SUBJECT: Presentation by ....

FORMAT GUIDELINES for
TEAM PRESENTATION OUTLINE

*I. Introduction

   A. Introduction of team

   B. General intro. of topic/purpose and what your
       presentation will be covering

   C. Attention-getter

*II. Content Areas
   A. List your first major point/content area and outline
       with specific points and/or details for each
       1. sub point
       2. sub point, etc.

   B. Major point #2
       1. sub point

-include what visual aids will be used

*III. Summary/Wrap-up

   A. Review major points from part II
   B. Check for any questions from audience
   C. Thank your audience

   IV. List of all materials/equipment required

Article Synopsis Outline Format

Directions: Complete your article synopsis outline exactly as explained below in one page, use 12 pt. font. *Do not use complete sentences.* Include the same headings for each section as illustrated below: *Thesis Statement* and *Major Points*. Include your article (stapled to back) with your synopsis.

---

your name
title/author/date of article

I. Thesis
    A. Provide summary of article

II. Major Points
    A. First major point
        1. Provide brief explanation and/or examples

    B. Second major point
        1.

    C. Third major point, etc.
        1.

- **Check that you didn't use any complete sentences in your outline *(no filler words like "a", "an", "the", etc.)!***

Memo Format Quiz
20 pts.

Directions: **Place the correct answer to each question in the space provided.**

1. List the 4 headings used in a memo *in proper order*:

    (1) _____

    (2) _____

    (3) _____

    (4) _____

2. Memo headings should be *lower case* or *upper case*. (circle one)

3. Memo headings should be *single* or *double spaced*. (circle one)

4. Sentences within a paragraph in a memo should be *single* or *double spaced*. (circle one)

5. Paragraphs *are* or *are not* indented when using the block style. (circle one)

6. What is the key difference in the purpose/use of a memo vs. a business letter?
   (4 pts.)

   _____

   _____

Business Letter Format Quiz
20 pts.

Directions: **Answer each of the following questions about business letters by placing your answer in the space provided or circling the correct answer.**

1. Business letters are used for communications *outside* or *inside* the Company. (circle one)

2. The inside address should be _____ line(s) below the dateline.

3. The salutation should be _____ line(s) below the inside address.

5. Sentences <u>within</u> a paragraph are *single* or *double* spaced.   (circle one)

6. Spacing <u>between</u> paragraphs is *single* or *double* spaced. (circle one)

7. Paragraphs *are* or *are not* indented when using block format. (circle one)

8-9. The complimentary close should have _____ line(s) before and _____ line(s) after.

10. There should be _____ line(s) before any enclosure notation.

Punctuation Practice Test

Directions: Add, change, or delete punctuation as required to properly punctuate each of the following sentences, then indicate the change after each sentence, e.g. "remove comma."

1. I will be in the office on Monday, and at home on Wednesday.

2. The student's last question was "How soon can we leave"?

3. The contract was approved but the work was not completed.

4. All two, four, and five year programs were approved.

5. The discussion was about Jurassic Park, a book about dinosaurs.

6. Homestead, Utah is the site for the next conference.

7. Will you please call me.

8. The team had an outstanding, first season.

9. On January 14, 1998 I entered the building.

10. Lauren was upset, she left her job.

11. The word stationery was spelled wrong.

12. The final points were allocated as follows: Ken, 150, Susan, 147, and Joe, 139.

13. She knelt beside the cold rushing water.

14. The survey found that three quarters of the participants were female.

15. The employee asked for a two week advance.

16. The contract was approved, however, the work was not completed.

17. A new uniform was issued, the old one was lost.

18. The equipment was not our's to use.

19. We plan on taking the bike, and the snowboard.

20. My dogs favorite toy was lost in the yard.

Punctuation Practice Test - Solution

1. *I will be in the office on Monday and at home on Wednesday.*
   (remove comma)

2. *The student's last question was "How soon can we leave?"*
   (quotation marks outside of punctuation)

3. *The contact was approved, but the work was not completed.*
   (add comma)

4. *All two-, four-, and five-year programs were approved.*
   (add hyphens)

5. *The discussion was about <u>Jurassic Park,</u> a book about dinosaurs.*
   (italicize or underline title)

6. *Homestead, Utah, is the site for the next conference.*
   (add comma)

7. *Will you please call me?*
   (add question mark)

8. *The team had an outstanding first season.*
   (remove comma)

9. *On January 14, 1998, I entered the building.*
   (add comma)

10. *Lauren was upset; she left her job.*
    (add semicolon)

11. *The word* stationery *was spelled wrong.*
    (italicize or underline word reference)

12. *The final points were allocated as follows: Ken, 150; Susan, 147; and Joe, 139.*
    (add semicolons)

13. *She knelt beside the cold, rushing water.*
    (add comma)

14. *The survey found that three-quarters of the participants were female.*
    (add hyphen)

15. *The employee asked for a two-week advance.*
    (add hyphen)

16. *The contract was approved; however, the work was not completed.*
    (add semicolon)

17. *A new uniform was issued; the old one was lost.*
    (add semicolon)

18. *The equipment was not ours to use.*
    (remove apostrophe)

19. *We plan on taking the bike and the snowboard.*
    (remove comma)

20. *My dog's favorite toy was lost in the yard.*
    (add apostrophe)

CHECKLIST FOR THE "C's" OF BUSINESS COMMUNICATION

Before handing in a written assignment, please check the assignment carefully using the following checklist:

- CONSIDERATION/CHARACTER/CONFIDENCE: Lots of "YOU" attitude. Check the "empathy index." The use of "you" should outweigh the use of "I, me, my, we, us," or any other form of first person.

- CONCISENESS/CONCRETENESS: Be specific; get to the point; avoid wordiness.

- CORRECTNESS/COMPLETENESS: Be certain English mechanics are in place (correct spelling, correct punctuation, correct word usage, no words omitted, standard usage, format). Writers must provide all the details.

- CONVERSATIONAL TONE: Write as you speak; be positive; avoid clichés, redundancies, and idioms; do not overuse euphemisms.

- CLARITY: Be certain your writing is clear and unmistakable. Check for the following:

  o **Rule of primacy.** Items that are most important are placed first in the sentence or the paragraph; that is, to the **left** of the verb. The first paragraph is the most important.

  o **Rule of recency.** The second-most important item is place near the **end** of the sentence or the paragraph. The last paragraph is the second-most important paragraph.

  o **Guidelines for the use of demonstrative pronouns.** Define demonstrative pronouns by placing a noun after the demonstrative pronoun. Demonstrative pronouns are "this," "that," "these," and "those."

  o **Guidelines for expletives.** Expletives are "it," "there are," "there is." Avoid using expletives especially at the beginning of the sentence. Place the most important item to the left of the verb.

  o **Guidelines for "impressive" words.** Avoid using words designed to "impress" the reader. Use short words. The job of the writer is to "communicate,"—not "educate."

  o **Guidelines for sentences and paragraphs.** Use short sentences and short paragraphs for greatest emphasis.

Invoking the Rule of Primacy and the Rule of Recency

An expletive is a meaningless word—a word that adds nothing to the sentence or a word that does not provide clarity in the sentence. Some examples of expletives that you should use with caution in writing are *it is, it was, there is, there are,* and others. Rewrite the following sentences that will eliminate the expletives and will invoke the *rule of primacy.*

1. *It is* your reputation at stake.

2. *It is* essential for employees to be able to write clearly.

3. *There are* many people in today's society who feel that way.

4. *It is* important to learn how to write properly using a business format.

5. *It is* an important skill in the business world today, and *it* should be developed by everyone.

6. *There is* a lot to be learned about business writing.

7. *It is* a good possibility your writing skills will land you your first job.

8. One can never be a good enough writer; and with all *its* benefits, one should take a serious interest in *it.*

9. Communication, no matter what form *it* may be, is very essential in the world we live in today.

10. *It is* up to the businessperson to write the reports.

11. Many business students feel that *it is* not important to have knowledge of English skills.

Invoking the Rule of Primacy and the Rule of Recency

1. Your reputation is at stake.

2. To be able to writer clearly is essential for employees.

3. Many people in today's society feel that way.

4. Learning how to write properly using a business format is important.

5. Writing is an important skill in the business world today and should be developed by everyone.

6. A lot is to be learned about business writing.

7. Your writing skills will possibly land you your first job.

8. Communication, no matter the form, is very essential in the world we live in today.

9. Writing the reports is up the businessperson.

10. Many business students feel that having a knowledge of English skills is not important.

DEFINING DEMONSTRATIVE PRONOUNS

A demonstrative pronoun is one that points out (demonstrates) something or somebody. Demonstrative pronouns include *this, that, these,* and *those.* To provide clarity in your writing, **place a <u>noun</u> after a demonstrative pronoun.**

Those are mine. (lacks clarity)
Those books are mine. (provides clarity)

This will help reduce misunderstanding. (lacks clarity)
This plan will help reduce misunderstanding. (provides clarity)

Those are mine. (lacks clarity)
Those suggestions are mine. (provides clarity)

Please give *these* to the sales manager. (lacks clarity)
Please give *these reports* to the sales manager. (provides clarity)

Exercises: **Define the demonstrative pronouns in each of the following sentences. Use any noun that makes sense.**

1. These belong to the office manager.
2. That is my uncle.
3. This is quite interesting.
4. Are you one of those who works more than 40 hours a week?
5. Please hand me that.
6. Please give those to Magda.
7. This is the reason for the extremely large salary gap.
8. This will leave you in a very strange position.
9. Will you please hand me those so that I can finish the job.
10. Please see whether this is necessary in the business world.

Answers:

1. These *plans* belong to the office manager.
2. That *man* is my uncle.
3. This *insurance policy* is quite interesting.
4. Are you one of those *employees* who works more than 40 hours a week?
5. Please hand me that *book.*
6. Please give those *copies* to Magda.
7. This *policy* is the reason for the extremely large salary gap.
8. This *exercise* will leave you in a very strange position.
9. Will you please hand me those *tools* so that I can finish the job.
10. Please see whether this *behavior* is necessary in the business world.

INSTRUCTIONS FOR PREPARING BUSINESS CARDS

I.   Designing your business card

    A.   Using creative software
- Follow the directions on your creative software to design a business card. Below is a list of some software titles that contain business card templates:

Microsoft ® Picture It! 2001	American Greetings ® CreataCard®
Microsoft ® Publisher	Broderbund ® The Print Shop ®
Microsoft ® Greetings Workshop	CorelDRAW (Trademark)
Microsoft ® Home Publishing	Sierra ® Print Artist (Trademark)

    B.   Using word processing program
- Word processing programs such as Microsoft Word are very powerful and provide many features useful in creating your business card
- MS Word provides many templates, including a business card template